HOW TO WRITE A BESTSELLER

9 Easy Steps to Write, Publish, Promote, and Profit from Your Book

Vikrant Shaurya

How to Write a Bestseller: 9 Easy Steps to Write, Publish, Promote, and Profit from Your Book

Copyright © Vikrant Shaurya (2024)

All rights reserved. No part of this publication may be reproduced, stored in a retrieval system, or transmitted in any form or by any means without the prior written permission of the publisher.

ISBN: 978-1-950336-70-8

Published by Authorsonmission.com

CONTENTS

HOW TO WRITE A BESTSELLER 1

INTRODUCTION 7

    The Publishing World Is Changing 9
    How to use this book 13
    So, You Want to Become a Bestselling Author…. 15
    Why this book might not be for you 17
    What This Book Will Not Cover 18
    Find Out What's Stopping You 19
    The Bestseller Journey 24

PHASE I – PRODUCE 26

    How to effortlessly write a book that readers enjoy reading 26
    Step 1 – Ideation 28
    Turn Your Idea into Reality 28
    Ideation: How to find your best, most profitable book idea 30
    Ideation: How to discover Your "Why" to keep you motivated throughout the journey 37
    Ideation: How to identify your target readers 41
    Ideation: How to create your hook using The Three-Part Hook Creation System 44
    Ideation: How to write a book outline using The Outline Quadrant in less than 30 minutes 48
    Key Takeaways: Step 1 - Ideation 55
    Step 2 – Writing 56
    Putting the pieces together: 3 easy steps 56
    Writing: How to fast-track your research 59
    Writing: How to write the perfect book title and subtitle that sells 64
    Writing: How to craft the ultimate book introduction 72
    Writing: How to write the book like a pro 75
    Writing: How to summarize the content with a well-written conclusion 77
    Writing: 11 Hacks to Defeat Writer's Block 79
    Writing: Alternatives to writing the book yourself 85

Key Takeaways: Step 2 – Writing 93
Step 3 – Editing 94
Polishing the diamond to bring out its beauty 94
Editing: How To Conduct A Developmental Edit - Checking The Meat And Potatoes 97
Editing: How to line edit - making sure every word counts 98
Editing: How to copy edit - ensuring accuracy and readability 101
Editing: How to proofread - one last round for good measure 103
Editing: How to hire an editor 105
Key Takeaways: Step 3 – Editing 108

PHASE II – PUBLISH 109

How to package, publish, and distribute your book in 3 simple steps 109
Step 4 – Positioning 111
Positioning your manuscript to make it irresistible 111
Positioning: How to create a book description to increase book sales 112
Positioning: How to write an acknowledgment to win hearts 119
Positioning: How to write an author bio to showcase your expertise 121
Positioning: How to Choose Your Author Picture to Gain Trust 124
Positioning: How to Assign an ISBN to Your Book 126
Key Takeaways: Step 4 - Positioning 128
Step 5 – Design 129
Creating a great-looking book 129
Design: How to design your Kindle book cover to sell 131
Design: How to make a Paperback cover that will stand the test of time 138
Design: How to format your eBook to keep your readers engaged 142
Design: How to design a captivating Paperback layout 144
Design: How to design your Author website to establish your authority 150
Key Takeaways: Step 5 - Design 155
Step 6 – Distribution 156
Getting your book out there 156
Distribution: How to navigate Amazon's Kindle Direct Publishing (KDP) 158
Distribution: How to find the most profitable Amazon categories 161
Distribution: How to maximize your book's visibility with keywords 166
Distribution: How to publish your Kindle and Paperback books with an

easy step-by-step guide _____ 173
Distribution: How to publish an audiobook in 3 easy steps _____ 190
Key Takeaways: Step 6 - Distribution _____ 198

PHASE III – PROFIT _____ 199

How to launch the book to bestseller, get sales and reviews, and then monetize from the book _____ 199
Step 7 – Launch _____ 202
Essential campaign elements to launch your book successfully _____ 202
Launch: How to create your Author Page to Establish Your Authority 203
Launch: How to get initial book reviews _____ 206
Launch: How to make your book a #1 bestseller - a step-by-step blueprint _____ 208
Launch: How To Get 2x More Sales And Downloads For Your Book _____ 214
Launch: How To Get 100+ Reviews To Boost Book Sales _____ 220
Key Takeaways: Step 7 - Launch _____ 226
Step 8 – Marketing _____ 227
Getting your book into the minds of your potential readers _____ 227
Marketing: How To Get The Media Buzzing About Your Book _____ 228
Marketing: How To Land Podcast Appearances To Promote Your Book To A Mass Audience _____ 230
Marketing: How To Market Your Book On Social Media With Seven Best Practices _____ 236
Marketing: How To Run Amazon And Facebook Ads To Get 5x Book Sales _____ 242
Marketing: How To Collaborate With Influencers For Bulk Sales _____ 270
Key Takeaways: Step 8 - Marketing _____ 275
Step 9 – Monetization _____ 276
7-figure business models to build around your book _____ 276
Monetization: How To Leverage Your Book To Land Speaking Engagements _____ 277
Monetization: How To Generate High-Quality Leads Using Your Book 281
Monetization: How To Set Your Book Up To Win New Business For You _____ 284
Monetization: How To Create A Profitable Video Course Around Your Book _____ 288
Monetization: How To Develop Your Own High-Ticket Coaching

Program _____ 294
Key Takeaways: Step 9 – Monetization _____ 298

THREE MORE REASONS TO SELF-PUBLISH YOUR BOOK TODAY _ 299

Help Me Help Others With This Book _____ 301

CONCLUSION _____ 302

What's Next? _____ 304
How To Write A Bestseller _____ 305
Your FREE Gift _____ 310
About the Author _____ 312

INTRODUCTION

If I had to describe this book in a single sentence, it would be *"the fastest and easiest way to write, publish, and launch a book as a bestseller and then use its bestselling status to build a brand, get paid speaking gigs, and more clients."*

According to surveys in both the New York Times and Forbes, 81% of Americans aspire to write a book, although the tough reality is that only about 3% ever finish, and only about 1% actually publish their book. Shocking, I know! But I know you picked up this book because you are serious about writing, publishing, and, more importantly, profiting from your book. My goal is to help you get there!

Until Amazon launched its Digital Text Platform, now known as KDP, in 2007, traditional publishing was the only route available to authors for getting their books to market. However, going the traditional publishing route can take a long time to write, publish, and market a book. For example, Brendon Burchard's first book, *Life's Golden Ticket,* took him years to even land a publishing agent. And after he did and the book was finally published, it did not do very well at first. It was only with his next three books, all becoming *New York Times* bestsellers, that he was able to gain any traction in the publishing world.

With my help, you won't have to wait three years for your book to be written, published, and become a bestseller. I can make it really easy for you to get your book out there.

You may be wondering why I am so confident that I can help you.

After helping thousands of clients on their publishing journey through my company, Authors on Mission, I have learned the secrets to writing a really good book that your readers enjoy, then designing, publishing, marketing, and how to profit from your book. I will share all of them with you!

In *How to Write a Bestseller*, I will provide a step-by-step process to turn your book idea into a book, publish and promote it to bestseller status, and then how to use it to earn more than royalties. I will show you how to build a brand, get media coverage, and position yourself as a subject matter expert to gain new clients.

This simple and easy-to-follow guide will be your author's blueprint, opening the door to everything you can dream of.

The Publishing World Is Changing

If you've ever considered publishing a book, you may have wondered whether to go the Traditional or Self-publishing route. Both options have their advantages and disadvantages. But which path to choose depends on who you are.

As I've said, it's really hard to get an offer from a publishing label in traditional publishing. Unless you fall into any of the categories of people listed below, attempting that route is not recommended and, for many people, may deter them from becoming a published author.

- Celebrities
- Famous athletes
- A-List actors
- Household name CEOs
- Politicians
- Well-known writers

Now, just because you don't fit into one of those categories does not mean that what you have to say or share with the world is not valuable. For the majority of the people in the categories below, self-publishing is the way to go:

- Business owners
- Consultants
- Entrepreneurs
- C-level executives
- Financial planners
- Coaches
- Experts
- Speakers
- Anyone who wants to write a book

Why?

Let's start by comparing the pros and cons of both methods.

Traditional Publishing

Pros:

- Most publishing companies offer advance payment to the authors before the publishing process starts.
- The investment comes from the publisher's pocket, not the author.
- You have a good potential for getting traditional media coverage.
- There are more chances to display your book in bookstores.

Cons:

- A traditional publishing deal is like finding a needle in a haystack, with less than 1% of proposals being accepted for publishing.
- The processing time is very lengthy.
- The publishing company owns the rights to the book and keeps most of the royalties.
- The author has no marketing control.
- The publisher can change the content and design it according to its preference.
- Niche books are not accepted.
- It's almost impossible to make changes to the book once it's published.

And here's a myth-buster for you: The publishing company won't market your book. You actually need to do it yourself.Self-Publishing

Pros:

- Self-published authors retain all the rights and royalties of their book.
- The book is customizable according to the author's preference, including content, design, and ideas.
- The timeline works according to the author's pace.
- The author is free to make all the decisions, especially on the creative and marketing aspects.
- The author has higher profit returns.
- It's very easy to make changes to the book even when the book is published and live.
- In self-publishing, niche books are great because they target a very specific, well-defined audience, helping authors establish themselves as experts in that niche market.

Cons:

- If you're the author, you have to ensure the book is flawless from cover to cover. If done unprofessionally, it will reflect poorly on your reputation as an author.
- You need time to learn and manage the publishing process.
- Hiring the best team of professionals to work on your book might be too expensive.
- You can choose to spend either more money or more time working on your book.

Between the two options, you'll notice that self-publishing has weightier pros and fewer cons. The self-publishing method is much more customizable and author-friendly compared to traditional publishing, building your network and promoting your brand in the fastest way possible. And with the technology available to you through Amazon's KDP program, it is now easier than ever for everyone, no matter the position, niche, or subject, to become a published author and, more importantly, to make it to the top of the bestsellers list.

When it comes to income potential, self-published authors get maximum royalties and have more opportunities to build bigger businesses after their book comes out.

If you have decided to go for traditional publishing, I'll warn you now that half of this book will not be relevant because it discusses strategies specific to self-publishing.

How to use this book

Using this book is like using a map with the destination being bestselling author status. Here's a list of ways to maximize this book's full potential:

- Treat this as your publishing bible. Each section or phase will include actionable steps, Pro tips, and resources. I have also included an easy-to-read Key Takeaways section at the end so that you can come back any time and get a little refresher without reading the entire chapter again.

- Rather than reading the book cover to cover, I recommend reading it in sections, following through with the action items on the checklist provided, and then reviewing the Key Takeaways before moving on to the next section.

- Download the printable version of *The 1-Page Bestseller Checklist* from Authorsonmission.com/resources and stick it to your wall. I'll explain this in more detail in an upcoming chapter.

I assure you that by following the detailed instructions I will lay out in this book, you will be well on your way to writing, publishing, and launching your bestselling book like thousands of clients who have worked with me and my team.

But I also know that sometimes things happen, and you may not be completely satisfied with the results after giving it your best shot. Here is my guarantee: If you try everything in this book and cannot become a bestselling author, email me directly at vikrant@authorsonmission.com — and I will give you your money back. I'm totally serious!

Vikrant Shaurya, Founder and CEO of AuthorsOnMission.com

Are you ready? Let's get started.

In the following pages, I will share how I learned to write, publish, and market my first book, turning the first into many, and starting my journey in helping others become bestselling authors and grow their income, impact, and influence. The book will be divided into three phases:

- Phase I: Produce - How to effortlessly write a book that readers enjoy reading.

- Phase II: Publish – How to package, publish, and distribute your book in 3 simple steps.

- Phase III: Profit – How to launch the book to a bestseller, get sales and reviews, and then monetize from the book.

In each phase of the book, I will provide detailed step-by-step instructions on how you can go from an idea to having a printed book in your hands to propelling your book title to the top of the bestseller list and monetizing its bestselling status to attract new clients and media attention, build your brand, and earn more revenue.

So, You Want to Become a Bestselling Author....

As mentioned earlier, both Forbes and the New York Times have noted that 81% of Americans want to write a book. But only a small percentage, about 1%, of those people actually do. And an even smaller number become bestselling authors.

Motivational speaker Brian Tracy has stated, "If you want to establish your *author*ity in your industry, then you should become an *author*." Note the word author as the root of authority.

People want to become bestselling authors for many reasons, and, of course, there are a lot of benefits once you have accomplished this commendable feat.

Here are some of those benefits:

- **Title** – There's just something about the title "bestselling author." It has a nice ring to it, and it gives you a boost in confidence. If you have the title "bestselling author" in your resume, you have an edge over people who are just authors or don't even have a book at all.

- **Credibility** – Becoming a bestselling author validates your skills as a writer or as an expert in your field. It is a legitimate title that will make people trust you. Plus, it feels like a gold medal for all the hard work you've put into what you do.

- **Sales** – Once you become a bestselling author, you won't have any trouble selling your future books. People's doubts will be erased; they will trust you more and will want to learn more from you.

- **Higher pay** – Regardless of whether it's an author or non-author gig, you can charge more for your services because you already have results and numbers to back them up.

- **More opportunities** – Your bestseller can be a gateway to more author and non-author opportunities like:
    o Paid speaking engagements
    o Getting high-paying clients
    o New businesses
    o A continuous pipeline of leads
    o Creating and selling a video course on your book's topic
    o Getting high-ticket clients by selling a coaching program

If these opportunities interest you, then keep reading. The last chapter of this book is dedicated to how to use your bestselling book to monetize and do all the things above.

Why this book might not be for you

While this book is designed to help a wide range of people write, publish, and market their books, there are a few exceptions to know about. For example, this book might NOT be the right choice if you:

- **Write fiction** – This is a manual for nonfiction books.
- **Want to do it all by yourself** – If you don't want an easy-to-apply guide and prefer to do the heavy lifting on your own, you don't need this book.
- **Have no reason to be an author** – If you're just reading for fun, then this is not the book for you.

If you have a reason to become a bestselling author of a nonfiction book and are looking for a straightforward, no-fuss guide to turning your ideas into a bestselling book, then I am happy you are here.

What This Book Will Not Cover

Most books on self-publishing fall into two problematic categories. The first category is too theoretical. It doesn't take into account the reality of what it's like to be a self-published author.

The second category is too motivational, talking about doing all of it without actually answering the question of "how." It's focused on the emotional side of things, the mindset, without the actual advice.

This book is different from those two because it's a take-you-by-the-hand guide to becoming a bestselling author, all the way from generating your book idea from scratch to turning it into a bestselling book and then how to monetize your new bestselling author status. This book will be by your side throughout your publishing journey.

Another benefit of reading *this* book is that I have been where you are and am more than willing to pass everything I have learned to *you*! Also, I have helped thousands of clients through my company... Authors On Mission...and I am going to share all the secrets in this book.

I will go straight to the point of teaching you the step-by-step strategies to turn your idea into a published book with actionable examples.

Ultimately, you will walk away knowing how to write, publish, promote, and profit from your book in just nine easy steps, leveraging it to maximize your success.

Find Out What's Stopping You

So, we talked about why you may want to write a book and the benefits of becoming a bestselling author. But the sad reality is that many people have great ideas for a book and want to be authors, but they don't push through and make it happen.

Why?

What has been holding you back from writing a book before now? The only logical answer in my mind is that you did not have the tools to make it happen. And that's where I come in.

But before we dive into the details of the step-by-step process, we must first take a quick look at some other possibilities.

Here are the common fears that hold back aspiring authors from sitting down and writing their books:

- *I have ideas but don't know how to write.*
- *I don't have the time.*
- *I've started a book but don't know how to finish it.*
- *I'm afraid my readers won't take me seriously.*
- *It takes years for a book to become a bestseller.*
- *I'm afraid people will think I'm a fraud.*
- *I'm worried my book might be a huge flop.*
- *I'm afraid this all might be a big waste of time.*

Feeling nervous and uncertain is normal when you don't know how to do something. I am assuming you know how to swim. If not, then when you learned how to drive a car or anything else, you didn't start off going to the deep end of the pool. However, once you did learn, you started going deeper and deeper, and now you can swim in the open ocean.

I want to encourage you that learning to write a book and the steps to make it to the top of the charts is a process, just like everything else. You didn't wake up one day and were automatically an amazing swimmer.

It took hard work, diligently working toward your goal, and following the instructions of your coach, mentor, or instructor. Well, consider me as your coach throughout this process, too.

Through the years and in working with more than 10,000 clients, I have observed many authors and entrepreneurs fall behind, not publishing their books for some of the following reasons:

1. Impostor Syndrome

Authors hear a voice in their head that says, "What if people won't buy my book?" Or "People will say bad things about my book or leave bad reviews." "What if I will not be able to finish my book?" Believing that voice whispering to them is what's known as the Impostor Syndrome.

It's normal for first-time authors to feel this way. Even the big names, such as Neil Gaiman, a bestselling and award-winning author, and Maya Angelou, a writer for more than 50 years, experienced this, too.

The best way to overcome this is to acknowledge that Impostor Syndrome is making you think this way and that those lies you are telling yourself are holding you back from following through.

2. Analysis Paralysis

This is the state of overthinking to the point that you never decide or act at all. Some authors find it overwhelming to choose an option, or sometimes they over-complicate decisions when it's supposedly a simple one.

The best thing to do is to take the first step and find your 'Why' to write your book. As discussed in the early part of this book, "Why" serves as a guide in writing your book. It gives you a sense of direction as you move forward.

All the other steps are those you've just read about, from the book outline to the writing all the way to designing and even marketing.

These steps have already been used for years and have produced successful authors.

All you must do is follow them and trust the process.

3. Procrastination

Writers procrastinate for various reasons. Maybe they are afraid of failing? Maybe they don't like the way they write or maybe because they are just too busy?

When procrastination hits you, you should acknowledge that the habit of procrastination exists in you.

Find out when and how you procrastinate. Break down a big task into smaller tasks. If you are working on editing and it seems overwhelming, use the "5 Rounds of Editing" guide to help you.

Instead of editing everything in one go, do the content edits first, then the line-by-line edits, the verbal read-through, the copyediting, and then the proofreading.

That way, you will be able to polish your manuscript and not get overwhelmed with doing it all at one time.

4. Self-Doubt

"And by the way, everything in life is writable about if you have the outgoing guts to do it, and the imagination to improvise. The worst enemy to creativity is self-doubt." — Sylvia Plath

One of the things that I see very often and, in fact, have struggled with myself is doubting whether anyone would want to read something I wrote. Why do you doubt your abilities, life experience, and skills?

Remember that you have already come a long way to reach this point in your life. You may have even overcome something more challenging or overwhelming.

The decision to read this very book is already a huge leap forward in that direction. Keep a record of the good things that you have done and remind yourself of what you have already accomplished.

Push aside those thoughts that you are not good enough or that you can't do it and believe that you, indeed, can publish your own book. Everyone has something of value to say or share, and only you can bring it to the world.

5. Lack of Skills

I am here to tell you that you don't necessarily need to know how to write to be considered an expert or, as I said earlier, have something to say. English is not my first language, and frankly, my grades in English subjects during high school were not the greatest, yet I am still able to write this book. So, if English is not your first language, don't let that stop you. If I can do it, you can too!

You may think of an author as someone like Shakespeare, Ralph

Waldo Emerson, Maya Angelou, or JK Rowlings. And, of course, they are all considered excellent writers, but what about your writing isn't equally as terrific? What qualifies them as any better?

If your writing skills are a sticking point and you just don't believe you have the skills to get the job done, don't worry! I will provide another option to ensure you produce that bestseller even if your personal skills are not what you would consider bestseller quality.

While I don't profess to be a therapist or an expert in helping you overcome some of the emotional, mental, and/or psychological roadblocks you may encounter, I want to help you achieve your goal of writing a book and becoming a bestselling author.

This means being aware of these traps to avoid them before falling into them. If you find yourself at one of these pitfalls, it's not too late to pull yourself up and get back on track.

So, now that we have that out of the way, are you ready to begin?

The Bestseller Journey

After helping thousands of my clients go from book idea to bestseller, and after going through this journey with them thousands of times, I have created a very simple yet powerful 1-page Bestseller Checklist that we now use at our company, Authors On Mission, to help our clients in-house on their publishing journey.

This 1-page checklist has everything you need to go from book ideas to bestseller, and my goal is to simplify the entire publishing process, making it extremely easy for you to understand and follow.

I'd highly recommend you download this checklist, print it out, paste it on the wall in your workspace, and start checking the boxes as you complete each step.

I am certain this visible checklist will motivate you to keep moving forward.

Also, I have seen that one of the biggest reasons people are not able to write and publish their books is they have no clarity on what to do and what not to do. There are thousands of articles and YouTube videos, but they make the entire process more overwhelming and complicated.

But this 1-page bestseller checklist will make it easy for you to navigate the entire publishing process.

Here's what it looks like:

Produce

1. IDEATION
- Book Idea
- WHY
- Target Reader
- Hook
- Outline

2. WRITING
- Research
- Title & Subtitle
- Introduction
- Rough Draft
- Conclusion

3. EDITING
- Content Editing
- Line-by-Line Editing
- Verbal Read-Through
- Copyediting
- Proofreading

Publish

4. POSITIONING
- Description
- Acknowledgement
- Author Bio
- Author Photo
- ISBN

5. DESIGN
- Kindle Cover
- Paperback Cover
- eBook Formatting
- Paperback Formatting
- Book Trailer

6. DISTRIBUTION
- Amazon KDP Account
- Profitable Categories
- Profitable Keywords
- Kindle and Paperback on KDP
- Audiobook on ACX

Profit

7. LAUNCH
- Amazon Author Central
- Initial Reviews
- #1 Best-seller Spot
- More Sales and Downloads
- More Reviews

8. MARKETING
- Author Website
- Press and Media Coverage
- Social Media Marketing
- Paid Ads
- Influencers' Platform

9. MONETIZATION
- Speaking Opportunities
- Get New Clients
- Lead Generation
- Video Course
- Coaching Program

You can download a printable version of the "1-page Bestseller Checklist" at Authorsonmission.com/resources.

The 1-page Bestseller Checklist comprises three major phases: Produce, Publish, and Profit. Each phase is divided into three steps and further broken down into five sub-steps each.

This single-page document includes everything you need to write, publish, and launch your book. Let's dive in!

PHASE I - PRODUCE

How to effortlessly write a book that readers enjoy reading

"A book is simply the container of an idea—like a bottle; what is inside the book is what matters."

—Angela Carter

When I first decided to dip my toes into this unfamiliar territory of book writing, I faced many of the same fears or beliefs I spoke about earlier. Yet I pushed forward, now having multiple books under my belt and helping thousands of my clients write theirs.

I say that to reiterate that I am very familiar with the process and will share all of the secrets with you.

In fact, during my writing journey, I realized how very important this first phase, writing, is to the overall success of achieving my goal of leveraging my book to earn a profit. All the phases are important, but as the quote above indicates, it is what's inside that matters.

So, in the next pages, in the Produce Phase, I will walk you through the exact steps to help you create quality content. Of course, without quality content, you don't actually have a product to sell and get you to that bestselling author status.

We will go step-by-step from ideation to writing, including some Pro Tips for hiring a ghostwriter to editing.

By the end of this phase, you will have:

- Book outline or Table of Contents
- Book title and subtitle
- A completed manuscript

An edited final manuscript ready for publishing

STEP 1 – IDEATION

Turn Your Idea into Reality

The first step in writing a book is organizing your ideas. This will help you stay on track throughout the writing process because you know where you're going. This includes creating a clear outline to guide you along the way.

In this step, we will cover:

- How to find your best, most profitable book idea
- How to discover your "Why" to keep you motivated throughout the journey
- How to identify your target readers
- How to create your hook using The Three-Part Hook Creation System
- How to write a book outline using The Outline Quadrant in less than 30 minutes

But before we jump right in, I want to remind you, if I haven't already, that part of what will make your book a success is *you*! You have something unique to offer readers that will give them value, knowledge, information, insight, or motivation.

Some people will approach the next steps in the writing process based on their expertise, story, and knowledge. They may not necessarily need to identify the book idea but may need help narrowing the scope of the project. Others may be simply looking to find a book topic or idea without being an expert already in any one area. In this case, you will approach the process from a different perspective, trying to identify the most profitable topic or subject.

No matter what topic you write on...no matter what ways you pick to solidify your idea...your end goal should be to focus on the reader and how your book can be useful and add value to their life.

The key is to remember that you are not writing the book for yourself; you are writing the book for the reader. So always put your reader first, considering their pain, problems, and struggles. If you can successfully connect with them and share the game plan to overcome their struggles and pain points, then nothing can stop your book from being a success.

Ideation: How to find your best, most profitable book idea

I want to pause here for a moment to talk about the word "profitable." Like the word "success," being profitable is relative and depends on how you define it.

For example, after publishing my first book, I looked at my earnings report for the first month and discovered that I had made my first online income in the form of a royalty: $13. I was ecstatic. It was not that much, but I considered it a huge accomplishment already.

Then, in the next month, after doing some marketing, I made around $448.

In other words, the book writing process was profitable for me because I was in such a predicament that anything positive in my account was profitable.

I remember reading a story in a [Forbes article](#) about a self-published author who earned $450,000 per year in royalties. Did he have a profitable book idea?

All I am saying is that only you can determine what profitable is to you and note that it does not have to be from royalties. If you position it right, you can monetize it on the backend and make tons of money. As an example, Brooke Castillo started her career by writing books, but now she has built a $15M/year business while working just 3 days per week... and everything started from writing a book.

We will cover some amazing strategies on how to leverage your bestseller and convert it into revenue in the last chapter.

My goal is to provide you with all the tools and resources to achieve your goal, no matter what it is.

Now, back to the subject. Your book idea is the first important milestone you must accomplish in the book writing process. For you to come up with that perfect profitable book idea, you need somewhere to look first.

The following are just a few ideas depending on your approach, as discussed earlier.

1. Look at yourself.

Your life's story is an interesting topic. People want to know how you got to where you are.

Your humble beginnings, your struggles, and your breakthroughs are all potential chapters for your upcoming book. Topics that go into your passions and purpose will help others feel inspired and fulfilled.

Think about what kind of advice, suggestions, and actionable ideas you can offer to your readers. What topics are you passionate about?

Maybe it's a list of how-to's like: "How to_," "[Number] of ways to ," "How to_without doing._"

By following these formats, you give solutions to your readers' problems and why they should get hold of those ideas.

2. Look at your assets.

Another area to look for profitable book ideas is your social media accounts and websites. Look at your FB page and find out which of your posts had the most engagement. Check out the Page Insights and find out which ideas pique the interest of your readers.

If you own a self-hosted website, go to your cPanel Analytics program and look at the information about keywords. See which keywords drive the most traffic to your site.
Another tool to use is [Google Analytics](). This works best with your website SEO (Search Engine Optimization) and shows which keywords perform best. The numbers you see in these tools will help you see which ideas are profitable.

3. Ask your ideal readers.

If you want to find a topic with a lot of demand, ask people who are willing to pay for it. Get that valuable information from your target readers. To do this, you must have researched who your ideal reader is, which I will talk about in more detail in a bit.

The most profitable ideas are those that will address their problems, pains, goals, and desires. They want to know the answers to their problems, the relief for their pains, the way to reach their goals and desires.

If you focus on the issues that your ideal readers face, you can find a profitable book idea that will give them just what they need.

You can conduct an online survey, do one-on-one phone interviews, or create a poll on your social media groups.

You can post a question on forums like [Quora](#) or [Reddit](#) and see what topics people want to know more about. This will help you uncover which ideas are marketable to your target readers.

4. Spy on your competitors.

Another area to explore for book ideas is your competitors, assuming you have a general idea of the subject, genre, or industry. A competitor is someone who produces similar books, writes about similar topics, talks about the same ideas, or discusses similar subject matters.

Observe what they do and figure out how you can come up with a better version of it.

Of course, make sure that you do not plagiarize by taking their work and passing it off as your own. Stay ethical and be creative by finding a different angle to the topic.

You can give the idea a twist by adding your personal insights and experiences. You can also look at the reviews and comments on their products and services.

You can get inspiration by checking out the Read Sample feature on Amazon to see the main idea of your competitor's books.

Books › Business & Money › Job Hunting & Careers

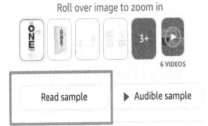

6 VIDEOS

Follow the authors

The ONE Thing: The Sur Extraordinary Results Ha

by Gary Keller (Author), Jay Papasan (Author)

4.6 ★★★★☆ ˅   19,403 ratings   **4.1** on

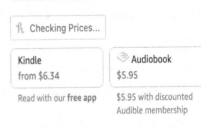

ℏ Checking Prices...

Kindle	Audiobook
from $6.34	$5.95
Read with our **free app**	$5.95 with discounted Audible membership

Save up to 8% with business pricing. Sign up for

What's your ONE thing?

People are using this simple, powerful concept t helping their employees be more productive wit Churches are conducting classes and recommen

By focusing their energy on one thing at a time
˅ Read more

▭ Report incorrect product information.

Print length	Language
1.	🌐
240 pages	English

Go to:

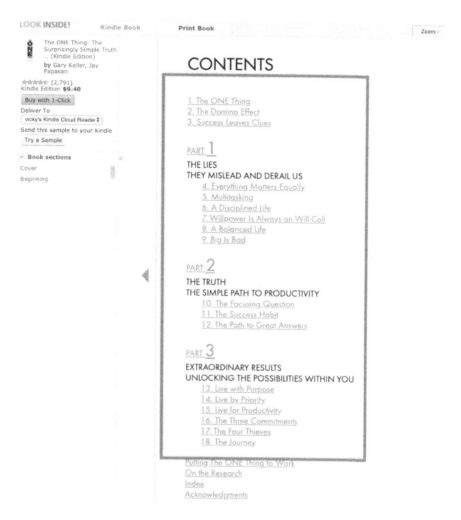

Know what things your competitors lack and find out how you can fill that gap. If this idea is working for your competitors, package it in a better way and earn more from it.

5. Research other people's ideas.

Learn from other people by creating a compilation of their ideas.

A collection of stories, jokes, quotes, interviews, mistakes, or step-by-step guides from other people can be the perfect book idea. And you don't have to do most of the writing. An example of this is Jack

Canfield's Chicken Soup for the Soul.

You can source material from influential people, remarkable events, or the most sought-after guides. Just come up with a main idea and then summarize your compilation.

Pro Tip: Make a list of book ideas that you have collected. Even if these are just rough ideas, writing them down gives more clarity down the line.

Rank your book ideas, looking at your expertise, your research, and any concept that may be new, exciting, and innovative.

Write your final book idea here:

Ideation: How to discover Your "Why" to keep you motivated throughout the journey

"He who has a why can endure any how." —Frederick Nietzsche

Your "why" for picking up this book and wanting to write a bestseller may be completely different from mine, as it should be. Each of us has our own motivations and reasons for doing everything in our lives. Why should the book writing process be any different?

Nevertheless, finding your "Why" and staying true to it will help you write a book that will bring tremendous value to your readers.

There are many reasons for writing a book. Here are some of the more popular "whys" I have discovered working with many clients over the years.

1. Help people who are going through a similar problem or experience.

Going through a difficult life experience and living to tell the tale is the kind of inspiring self-improvement book people love reading.

For example, in *You Are a Badass at Making Money* by Jen Sincero, she talks about how she cracked the code on earning a passive income—and she shares this knowledge with other women to help them overcome debt and gain financial freedom.

Do you have a proven solution to a problem that affects a lot of people (like money issues, for example)?

2. Build credibility, authority, or expert status.

Thought leadership is the business buzzword of the decade. We live in a time when it is no longer enough for leaders just to run businesses well. They also must show proof, in book form, of their trail-blazing success.

Virgin founder Richard Branson, now the author of more than 20 books, comes to mind as one of the most successful business magnates and authors.

Think about demonstrating your authority and originality by publishing a book to elevate your status from business leader to thought leader.

3. Share your distinctive point of view.

Do you have a deep interest in a topic or issue that is affecting the world at large? This kind of nonfiction book could be a real game-changer—one that will completely flip the way we view life as we know it.

For example, the book Outliers by Malcolm Gladwell has dominated the global conversation, continually changing the way we view learning and mastery for over ten years now.

4. Dominate a niche market.

Some successful nonfiction writers have built their success by filling a "gap" in the market.

Through consistent blog publishing, they have found an unfulfilled demand for books on topics that match their knowledge and expertise.

For example, Seth Godin's prolific nonfiction authoring career started as a blog on marketing for the digital landscape. He expanded his blog into a full book titled Purple Cow, which unleashed an ever-growing demand for his marketing brilliance.

5. Launch a career as a writer.

Transitioning to a writing career for the love of the craft is reason enough to write a series of books. The world needs writers now more than ever to tell stories, educate, entertain, and make sense of the world.

Bestselling author Simon Sinek switched from a lucrative advertising career to teaching leaders and organizations how to inspire people through his books and speaking events.

He is now known as a global leadership guru of the "start with why" movement.

6. Generate leads for your business.

Author and business leader Dan Lok published his first book just as he was getting his marketing consultancy business off the ground.

He gave away free copies instead of a business card or a brochure to win business prospects and earn their trust.

A dozen books later, Dan Lok runs thriving, multimillion-dollar businesses and is known worldwide as the leading expert in Internet marketing.

7. Get paid to speak.

Publishing a bestselling book leads to speaking opportunities to engage a global audience and get ideas to spread.

To promote her book, Daring Greatly, then little-known author Brené Brown spoke to a small audience at TedX; 11.4 million views later, Brené is now one of the most-watched TedX speakers of all time.

This success is proof of the power of a book to move audiences around the globe.

Those are just some of the most popular WHYs for writing a nonfiction book. You need to discover your own by asking yourself one simple question: Why do I want to be a published author?

From building your personal brand, generating leads, helping people, making money, or just for the sake of writing, your WHY can be anything that's powerful for you.

Whatever your reason is, be honest with yourself about it. Your WHY will be the fuel that keeps you going and inspires you every step of the way on your book-publishing journey.

So, what's your WHY?

Is it getting high-paying clients?

Generate high-quality leads?

Get paid to speak on more stages?

Receive social media attention and attract new clients?

Pro Tip: When you discover your "why," you will gain the courage to continue, the willpower to finish, and the motivation to persevere even when the going gets tough.

Ideation: How to identify your target readers

As you write your book, it is important to identify your target readers and persona, or in other words, the people you expect to read it. I assume you are not writing a book for it to simply sit on a shelf!

Whatever the reason you have started on this journey, the ultimate goal will be for readers to not only purchase and read it but also to share it with others who they believe will enjoy it as much as they did.

Thus, all the more reason to identify who those readers are and how to connect with them. Identifying your target readers can guide you in creating your content, ensuring you produce a book that someone will *want* to read.

Let's look at several things to consider.

Target demographic vs. target persona

A demographic is basically market data that defines the people who are most likely to be interested in reading your book.

They are classified by age, gender, ethnicity, education, income, profession, and family status.

A persona is a semi-fictional individual who represents your target demographic. Your target persona is further defined by lifestyle, behavior patterns, and motivations.

Why develop a target persona?

To download this Reader Avatar Worksheet, go to https://authorsonmission.com/resources.

While it is important to know the target demographic of your book, it helps to see beyond the stats and imagine them as a real person as you write, understanding their personality as a reader and focusing on what may inspire them to pick up a particular book.

Developing a target persona uses demographic data to bring your reader to life. This enables you to think about them more deeply, including their wants, needs, and motivations, and in turn, write more clearly and purposefully.

To create a profile of your target persona, consider some of the following:

- Fictional name: This helps humanize your target reader and forces you to think about someone specific when you write your book and develop the marketing for it.
- Gender
- Age
- Education
- Location
- Occupation

- Marital Status
- Background or Early Life
- Aspirations: What motivates them? What are their career aspirations? Their life goals?
- Goals and values: What is important to them?
- Challenges and Pain Points: What causes them pain? What stresses them out? What problems are they looking to solve?
- Hobbies and interests: What entertains them? How do they like to spend their free time?
- Objection and roles
- Where do they get their information? Do they listen to podcasts or read blogs? Are they avid readers, or do they prefer audio books?

I would highly recommend you download this Reader Avatar Worksheet, available at [AuthorsonMission.com/resources.](AuthorsonMission.com/resources)

Ideation: How to create your hook using The Three-Part Hook Creation System

A book's hook is a statement that makes readers interested in what you have to say. It will also be crucial in your introduction as you work to capture their attention and inspire them to keep reading.

Here are just some of the benefits of creating a strong hook:

1. Your hook can serve as your test of the market for interest and potential profitability. Post it on your blog, discuss it in conversations, or share it in a post and see how your friends, family, and followers react to it. That should give you a good indication of whether you are on to something worthwhile or if you should select another topic from your list.
2. Your book's hook serves as your writing navigator. When you're tempted to go off your main topic, the book's hook will keep you focused on the purpose of your book.
3. When your book has a great hook, it can catch a potential reader's attention. You give the readers a good reason why they should grab a copy of your book instead of another. You position your book to stand out in the marketplace.
4. As the author of the book, you also get to position yourself as the expert on the subject matter. Even if you're a new author, people will see you as someone who's bringing something interesting and valuable to the market. This will help you land speaking gigs, increase book demand, obtain high-ticket clients, and create other channels of income streams, like courses, workshops, mentorship, etc. Of course, all with the intention of fulfilling your "why."

The problem with writing a hook is some people tend to make the hook very complicated.

Some hooks are too vague and generic to help the book stand out.

Others are so long that they lose the readers' attention instead of retaining them.

When you create your hook, you want to follow just three simple rules: keep it short, specific, and unique.

To help you accomplish this goal, I have created a 3-Part Hook Generation system.

Below is a simple guide with real examples to help you get started.

Part 1 - What is the subject of your book?

No need to get fancy here. Just briefly describe what your book is about.

Here are a few great examples:

1. A book about working and living as a digital nomad.
2. A book about medical care done the right way.
3. A book about influencing people and winning friends.

Part 2 - What does your book promise?

Detail your book's intention for the reader in one brief statement. Using the same topics from above, list a description of the book's promise or value:

1. Escape the 9-to-5 and live and work anywhere.
2. Ensure professional excellence.
3. Make people instantly like you.

Pro Tip: This brief statement is often used as the book's subtitle.

Part 3 - Why does your book matter?

Describe your book's spark and explain the passion behind it. Think about why you're writing your book and why people should care about reading it.

Write out a clear statement on what the reader could take away from your book.

1. So that you can improve the quality of your life
2. So that more lives are saved than lost
3. So that you can have meaningful relationships

Finally, combine the three parts above to complete the hook of your book.

1. Write a book about life as a digital nomad, escape the 9-to-5, and live and work anywhere so that you can improve the quality of your life.
   (The 4-Hour Work Week)

2. Write a book about medical care done the right way and ensure professional excellence so that more lives are saved than lost.
   (The Checklist Manifesto)

3. Write a book about influencing people and winning friends to make people instantly like you so that you can have meaningful relationships.
   (How to Win Friends and Influence People)

ACTION ITEMS:

Complete the hook of your book by filling in the blanks in the right column.

1. I will write a book about:	
2. that promises to:	
3. so readers can:	

You can download a printable version of this Action Sheet at: Authorsonmission.com/resources

Ideation: How to write a book outline using The Outline Quadrant in less than 30 minutes

Planning for your book outline is a rigorous process. I've seen people get stuck for months on this step as they expect to have all the ideas, concepts, and words written out.

I like to think of the outline as a brain dump of ideas, allowing you to free-flow thoughts in a way that is malleable, fluid, and organized.

I know that it can be frustrating and even a bit overwhelming to sit down and try to put all your thoughts on paper, so to simplify this process, I have created the Outline Quadrant. This process will help you create your book outline faster.

It should be considered a loose framework since as ideas about each topic begin to flow, the outline will expand and take on a new shape.

An outline (or the Table of Contents) is a roadmap that plots your book's journey. It also helps you to remain organized and visually see how the content will flow.

An outline can also be a guide as to the length of the end product, your manuscript. While you do not have to determine the exact word count you want to achieve at this point, it is a good idea to identify what type of product you want to create in general terms. Of course, the length of the final product will determine how much content is required, which also impacts the length and depth of your outline. Don't worry if this sounds really confusing! I'll go into more detail in Step 2 when we discuss writing your first draft.

Focusing on a working outline before you even begin typing a draft is important. Just like a map guiding you in the right direction, a detailed outline will give you the mental clarity and direction to combat writer's block, fight against the fear of the process, and quiet that voice whispering that you can't do it.

I want to share a little bit about how a detailed outline helps me in the process. Once I move on to the writing stage, I often use the outline to help me continue making forward progress. Writer's block is a very real phenomenon and does not reflect your capabilities or skills. Even the most prolific writers can sometimes have difficulty producing new work or find the free flow of ideas stifled. When I find myself in this position in a particular area or topic, I move on to another section of the outline, intending to return to the one I left once the creativity flows again. There is certainly no shame in the game. A detailed outline allows you the freedom to do this without losing a thought or missing a critical step.

As you see the words materialize on the paper and the ideas take shape, a good outline will put your mind at ease and make the actual writing process a pleasant experience.

The Outline Quadrant

Within Step 1, we have discussed the book idea, your why, your potential readers, and the hook, which will be used as important elements to write your book outline. If you need to go back and review those, now would be a good time for a refresher. But don't worry, I will give you some tips along the way.

This is how the Outline Quadrant looks:

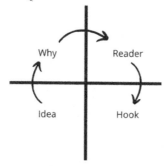

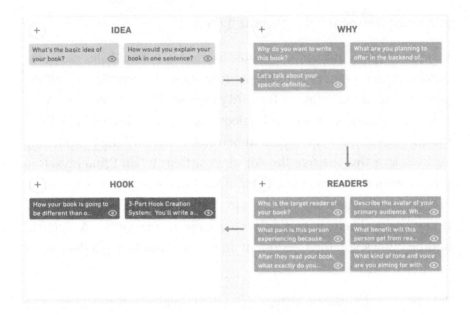

You can download a printable version of the blank Outline Quadrant at <u>Authorsonmission.com/resources</u>.

Download and print out the blank <u>outline quadrant.</u> Create your own Outline Quadrant and paste it on your wall with the four elements filled in.

Here's a recap of the four elements for easy reference while creating your Outline Quadrant:

Book Idea

Before you can start writing your book, you need to start with the BIG idea.

The book idea is the foundation of your book's outline. All major and minor ideas are generated from this BIG idea.

Start your book outline by considering the topics that surround your main idea. What topic do you want to talk about?

Write it at the top of your outline so you will remember to stick to your main idea.

Your "Why"

Your "why" dictates the direction of your book.

Think about the goal that you want to accomplish. In other words, "why" are you writing this particular book?

From here, you can come up with supporting chapters that close the gap between point A to point B. What value can your book give to your readers?

Here are some examples of WHYs and what topics you can add to your outline:

- If you want to help solve a problem that people are going through, you can share your solutions and actionable items so that other people can solve those problems, too.

- If you want to build your personal brand, you need to share something about yourself—your success story, life experience, etc.

- If you want to get more clients, then you need to share information about your business. Make sure you do not become too salesy or pushy; instead, tell about it indirectly and share how your service helped a client solve a problem.

Target readers

It is vital to keep your target readers in mind as you build your outline. Ultimately, your target reader is who you are writing it for. This will help you stay on track regarding:

- Language

This will determine whether your target readers will easily understand your book. This includes the language of the country, jargon, technical terms, and abbreviations.

- Voice

The voice of your book will tell you how your book should be read. Knowing your target's age range will help you choose the right words and tone. For example, do you want it to be casual, academic, professional, serious, humorous, empathetic, etc?

- Pain Point or Problems

The most important part of learning about your target readers is knowing their pain points and problems that you can solve with your book. When you mention their pains and struggles, you're letting them know that you understand them. This enables you to build an instant connection with your readers.

The hook of your book

The hook of your book is the elevator pitch that gives your readers the big reason why they should buy your book and what sets it apart from other books on the same subject.

Think about a sales page that's compressed in one section.

If a reader takes a glimpse of your book, your hook should catch their attention and draw them into reading the entire book.

As you create your book outline, think of an angle that makes your book distinctive from the rest of the market.

Write down all four elements (Idea, Why, Reader, Hook) on your Outline Quadrant and display it prominently on the wall in front of where you work.

So, let's start creating the outline itself, keeping the elements of the Outline Quadrant firmly planted at the front of your mind. Each element is important and will help you structure your outline correctly.

- Get a pen and a piece of paper or open a Word document or a notepad application.

- Start a 30-minute timer.

- Write all the main ideas that you can think of about your book's topic. Don't worry about the flow, grammar, or logical sequence. The point of this activity is to bring out every idea.

- You can also write stories, examples, and case studies for any idea. You don't need to explain them yet.

- Jot down all main ideas and sub-ideas that come to your mind until the 30-minute timer goes off.

And just like that, you have created your first book outline.

The next thing to do is to put the ideas in the order you see works best for a good flow of content. Note that nothing is written in stone, so the order of any of these ideas can easily be changed or rearranged as the manuscript takes shape. What you may think makes logical sense at this stage may not fit with the overall flow once the content is written.

Another suggestion is using ChatGPT to create your book outline using your Outline Quadrant elements. Be sure to use a prompt. For example, enter: "Here is some information about my book. Please use this information to create an in-depth, granular Table of Contents for this book." Then simply copy and paste each of the questions and answers into the ChatGPT prompt and watch as the system quickly and painlessly creates the outline for you. You can even specify how many subchapters you would like in each chapter. Why not use technology to make the writing process easier and certainly faster? I must reiterate here, though, that I do not recommend using AI beyond this point in the process. As quickly as artificial intelligence has come on the scene, publishing companies, and Amazon in particular, will be developing software to identify and prohibit AI-generated content. So, while it is an amazing tool for efficiency and effectiveness, be sure to follow the human route for the rest of the writing process.

Pro Tip: Use a mind-mapping app to organize the ideas according to relevance or a logical sequence. There are many mind-mapping tools out there in the market. You will need to do some research to see which works best for you, but on the resource page, you can find the mind-mapping tool I recommend for creating the book outline at Authorsonmission.com/resources.

Key Takeaways: Step 1 - Ideation

So, that brings us to the end of Step 1. As I mentioned at the beginning, I want you to use this book as a guide, performing each step and action along the way. By following each step accordingly, you will be able to accomplish your goal. I have proven this to be true time and again. That said, I want to briefly recap what we covered in this particular Step before moving on to Step 2.

In Step 1, Ideation, you will kick-start the writing process by crystallizing your idea:

- How to find your best, most profitable book idea.
- How to discover your "Why" to keep you motivated throughout the journey.
- How to identify your target readers.
- How to create your hook using The Three-Part Hook Creation System.
- How to write a book outline using The Outline Quadrant in less than 30 minutes.

If you have gotten this far, you are ready to move on to Step 2 and put all the pieces together. But if you have not completed these tasks, I urge you to finish these critical elements of the process before moving on to ensure that you create a final product you will be proud of that will skyrocket to the top of the charts.

On the other hand, if you are feeling stuck or need some guidance at this point in the process, be sure to contact me at

vikrant@authorsonmission.com.

STEP 2 – WRITING

Putting the pieces together: 3 easy steps

"Just get it down on paper, and then we'll see what to do with it." — Maxwell Perkins

When I started out on this journey to write, publish, and monetize a book, I had no writing skills whatsoever. In fact, as I mentioned, English is not even my first language. So, if anyone had forces working against them from the beginning, it was me! Yet I was determined and put my effort into writing that first book.

I went at the writing process in attack mode. Having nothing else to do since I quit college, I sat down and wrote for maybe 16 or 17 hours per day. Of course, I am not saying by any stretch of the imagination that you should do the same. I just want to share with you that I completed my first manuscript within twenty-one days. I was determined that if I was going to make this work, I was going to figure it out, so I put all my efforts into the process.

While I do not want to give you the impression that speed will produce a bestseller, there is something about momentum. I had the momentum going, so I figured, why stop?

As we go through this next section on all things related to writing, I want you to consider the benefits that continuous forward motion has not only on the ultimate goal but also in your confidence in yourself that you do have what it takes to become a bestselling author.

This step outlines the workflow and tasks to get your book's content together. In other words, we will be building on your outline to create a narrative. This is where we will lay the foundation and build upon it to share, engage, educate, and inspire the reader using research, stories, and examples and imparting your own knowledge where appropriate. This *is,* in essence, the meat of your product, which means we will also spend a significant amount of time and energy on this step.

If you follow this plan, you will effectively work through the most challenging part of the whole self-publishing process—writing the book!

In this step, we will cover:
- How to fast-track your research
- How to write the perfect book title and subtitle
- How to craft the ultimate book introduction
- How to write the book like a pro
- How to summarize the content with a well-written conclusion

While the research and book title/subtitle are critical components of your book, in this section, I will focus on the three primary steps of the writing process, including:

- Introduction
- Chapters
- Conclusion

It is also important to note that although we have been thus far talking about all the ways *you* can write a bestseller, this is not the only option. For those interested in hiring a ghostwriter for this portion of the book writing process, I will provide an overview and what you should look for when hiring someone.

First things first, you should decide on a writing tool for actually writing your manuscript. I'm sorry to say that the days of filling page upon page of a spiral-bound notebook are gone and no longer a viable option, especially if you are interested in becoming a bestselling author. Then again, you would not be reading this book, hoping to absorb all its valuable information, if you wanted to handwrite your manuscript!

Last but not least, before we dive in, I encourage you to set up your writing environment, removing any distractions and uncluttering your space. If you want to produce a bestselling book, you must think, act, and write like a bestselling author.

Writing: How to fast-track your research

Research is an important component of any book. Depending on your topic, you may already be an expert in that particular area. However, to ensure your readers are confident in your expertise, making them eager and willing to receive the information you are sharing, you want to add current data, references, other expert testimonies, and examples. You may also need to fill some gaps where you may not be knowledgeable of recent trends, existing policies, or changes.

This confidence in your credibility will assist you later when we talk about marketing and promotion. Readers will share and write reviews when they believe what you are saying and how you delivered it.

On the other hand, if you are unfamiliar with the topic or maybe writing in a niche you have identified as profitable, you will need to learn more to write about the subject appropriately.

The only reason you should skip the research phase is if your book is entirely based on your own life experience because you can't exactly research your own life.

The bottom line is that research is important regardless of your knowledge of the subject matter, so this is not something you should skip over.

For some people, just the thought of doing research may make them want to run for the hills or derail the process. While there is no one way to craft a research plan, there are several strategies I recommend and have used myself to raise your research game.

But before I share those, let me tell you the kind of research you will have to do and, therefore, the research questions will vary depending on the intention of your book, the target readers, and, of course, the topic.

Strategies to up your research game

1. Keep your research questions in mind.

Your research questions help narrow your focus and save you time and energy. This will serve as your guide all throughout your research.

Here are just a few generic questions to get you started:

- What information do I need?
- How do I find a trusted source of information?
- Can I ethically use the information?
- Where do I find this information?

2. Use keywords to do a targeted Google search.

Use keywords to see what turns up in Google and review the results according to relevance.

3. Use a bibliography to mine for information.

Sometimes, you just need one solid book source and a little more material from the same book's bibliography. Check out the list of book references at the back for relevant titles.

4. Use multimedia sources.

Watching and listening to documentaries, movies, podcasts, and audiobooks is the fastest and easiest way to soak up information on your topic.

5. Use the cloud to get organized.

Organize bookmarked web resources on your browser and store

downloaded files on your Google Drive for quick and easy access.

6. Use forums and social media to connect with subject matter experts.

When in doubt, reach out to experts and other writers on the subject for a quick chat or interview.

7. Use content from your archive.

Here's a list of content pieces that writers repurpose or recycle as material for their books:

- Audio and/or video – interviews, podcasts, talks, lectures
- Social posts
- Blog posts
- Articles for established media outlets
- Presentation decks
- Academic research
- Industry white paper
- PowerPoint presentations
- Journals
- Reviews or testimonials
- Notes from books
- Highlighted quotes from favorite authors

Borrowing this approach from published writers, look into your own archive for similar information. Organize them into neat folders on your PC or in the cloud.

Then, review all the published and unpublished material and see if you can put together what could already be great content for the book you're about to write.

8. *Set a clear deadline to complete your research.*

Stay focused and commit to an end date for your research because if you are not careful, research can lure you into a rabbit hole and distract you from getting started on your book.

Lastly, in keeping with strategies to up your research game, I have compiled a list of AI tools to help fast-track your efforts:
- Scite.ai
- Elicit
- Scite.ai

Pro Tip: Be sure that if you are referencing any information that is not your own, such as data, statistics, a specific quote, surveys, or research, you must give credit by citing where the information was derived. I have created a handy checklist to help ensure you do not fall into the trap of plagiarism or not citing appropriately.

ACTION ITEMS:

Fill in this form and use it as a quick guide for organizing your research material. This information will also help you create your bibliography later.

RESEARCH QUESTION OR TOPIC	
TITLE OF THE SOURCE	
LINK TO THE SOURCE	
PAGE NUMBER/S	
AUTHOR	
DATE OF PUBLICATION	
TOP-LINE INFORMATION FROM THIS SOURCE	
QUOTATIONS FROM THIS SOURCE (IF ANY)	

You can download a printable version of this Action Sheet at Authorsonmission.com/resources.

Writing: How to write the perfect book title and subtitle that sells

Deciding on your book title is the most critical piece of marketing strategy. Your book will live or die on your chosen title once published. Period.

However, I don't want to scare you or detour you from your mission of writing the manuscript. Of course, nothing is set in stone, so the title and subtitle can be changed later in the process. But keeping the title in mind as you write serves as a mental anchor to help you stay on point. A title keeps you focused on creating a manuscript that makes sense and delivers on its promise.

For our purposes, let's call it a "working title."

You may wonder how you can choose the title without writing the book. But if you have a solid outline, you should be able to craft a book title relatively easily.

So, why is the title so important? The title is the first glimpse your target reader will get of your book, so you want it to be good.

My experience in publishing hundreds of books at authorsonmission.com has educated me on the psychology of the book-reading market. I have come to understand what potential buyers consider when choosing a book. This goes back to understanding your target persona and their unique reading preferences.

When deciding to buy a book, readers evaluate:

1. The book title
2. The book cover
3. The book description

4. The book reviews
5. The author bio
6. The book's first sentence or paragraph
7. The book's price

Of course, a good title does not guarantee your book's success. But a bad title will most definitely kill it.

Qualities of a winning book title

1. Attention-grabbing

A bad title is unremarkable. Like stale chips, they are boring and tasteless. A great title stands out and draws people's attention by being provocative, controversial, and/or presenting an exciting promise. For example:

Provocative - THE SUBTLE ART OF NOT GIVING A F*CK
Promising - THE 4-HOUR WORK WEEK
Controversial - FIRST BREAK ALL THE RULES

2. Easy to remember

A successful book title grabs attention and holds it. Think about how your book title stands out from all the information flooding the market, just like the catchiest songs and slogans from ads. You remember them because they leave an impression.

3. Searchable

A book title that's easy to remember should also be easy to type into a search bar (of Amazon). The easier it is to type correctly, the more likely it will turn up as an exact search result for your book.

4. *Short*

A short title makes a book attention-grabbing and easy to remember and also makes for a more visually appealing book cover.

5. *Informative*

An effective book title gives you an idea of what the book is about right off the bat. Just from reading the title, the potential buyer should be able to form an impression of what your book has to offer.

How can a good title be both short and informative?

Your short main title can be supported by a subtitle that briefly explains the idea behind the book. Below are examples of great one-word book titles with strong subtitles:

- RANGE: Why Generalists Triumph in a Specialized World
- OUTLIERS: The Story of Success
- GRIT: The Power of Passion and Perseverance

Most first-time authors often write a long-winded title to tell the reader what the book is all about. This is fine for a working title or a draft.

But, as with all writing, editing is necessary for crafting the perfect title. Work on refining and testing your title until you get it right.

Crafting the perfect title – a few ideas to get you started

1. *A clever turn-of-phrase*

- This style could be memorable because it suggests to the reader that the book is exciting, engaging, and original. For example:CRUSHING IT

- NEVER SPLIT THE DIFFERENCE
- BILLION DOLLAR WHALE

2. *A promise of value*

A title that presents achievement or a picture of a successful outcome checks off all the qualities mentioned above.

- I WILL TEACH YOU TO BE RICH
- THE TOTAL MONEY MAKEOVER
- SECRETS FOR CLOSING A SALE

3. *A thesis statement*

Draw in the right kind of reader by boldly stating your idea or position on issues that affect the world.

- THIS CHANGES EVERYTHING: Capitalism vs Climate
- YOU'VE GOT 8 SECONDS: Communication Secrets for a Distracted World

4. *A niche target*

Outrightly describe the book with the title to let the target readers know your book is designed for them.

- WHAT TO EXPECT WHEN YOU'RE EXPECTING
- ACCOUNTING FOR NON-ACCOUNTANTS

5. *A numbered guide*

- 48 LAWS OF POWER
- THE 7 HABITS OF HIGHLY EFFECTIVE PEOPLE
- HOW TO TALK TO ANYONE – 92 LITTLE TRICKS

6. *A curious expression*

- WHO MOVED MY CHEESE?
- LEAN IN
- SHOE DOG

7. *A straightforward challenge*

- DARE TO LEAD
- HOW TO MANAGE YOUR MONEY WHEN YOU DON'T HAVE ANY
- GETTING PAST 'NO'

8. *A templated format*

Sometimes, it pays to do the tried-and-tested title tropes. Try filling in the blank of any of the following examples to complete the book title:

- *THE SECRETS TO –*
- *THE ART OF –*
- *THE SCIENCE OF –*
- *THE JOY OF –*

- *CONFESSIONS OF –*
- *A JOURNEY TO –*
- *FINDING YOUR –*
- *KNOWING YOUR –*
- *ON THE SUBJECT OF –*
- *A BRIEF HISTORY OF –*
- *THE LIFE AND TIMES OF –*
- *HOW TO –*

Pro Tip: I can assure you that among the thousands of authors I have worked with, more than a handful of them have published a title different from the one they originally intended. Although the title is meant to keep you focused by design, sometimes a more appropriate title may develop organically from the content, better attracting your target readers.

Writing a subtitle

If the title is what attracts your target reader to your book, the subtitle is the "hook" that keeps them interested. It is the supporting statement that articulates the premise of the book.

Your nonfiction probably needs a subtitle if you tell people the title of your book, and they don't immediately get what it's about.

A good subtitle answers readers' questions when they encounter your book for the first time, such as:

What is this book about? Who is it for?
What does it promise?

Here are a few great examples of books with long subtitles that let readers know what they are getting into:

- EAT, PRAY, LOVE: One Woman's Search for Everything Across Italy, India, and Indonesia
- SELL LIKE CRAZY: How to Get as Many Clients, Customers and Sales As You Can Possibly Handle
- RICH DAD POOR DAD: What the Rich Teach Their Kids About Money That the Poor and Middle Class Do Not!

Pro Tip: As I mentioned in Step 1, the brief statement you deemed the "hook" can also be used as the book's subtitle.

Some final notes on crafting the title of your book

1. Book titles cannot be copyrighted.

Technically, you can call your book anything you want, including copying the titles of already published books.

While you are allowed to use any existing title from Harry Potter to The Holy Bible, this obviously does not make your book memorable, original, or searchable.

Also, copying an existing title is like falsely advertising your book. So it's not a good idea.

2. Book titles cannot be trademarked UNLESS ...

It is part of a series of books like Harry Potter or For Dummies how-to books. Or if a trademarked brand is part of the book title, like *Microsoft Excel™ For Dummies™*.

Below are some actionable steps to help you nail down your working title.

Pro Tip: Once you have created your Outline Quadrant, you can input those questions and content into ChatGPT and allow it to help you develop a compelling title and subtitle. Simply copy and paste the information into the prompt and allow AI to do its thing. You may also want to try it in Claude as well and see which one gives you a title and subtitle that will attract readers.

ACTION ITEMS:

Write 3 to 5 Book Titles and Subtitles in order of preference, with Number 1 as your favorite title. Short-listing your options helps with decision-making.

If you're still undecided, you can get a poll out on social media or split-testing sites like Pickfu. It will also help create early buzz for your book project.

Example:

Dear friends, I'm working on a book. Can you help me decide on a title? Which of the following resonates the most with you?

1.

2.

3.

4.

5.

You can download a printable version of this Action Sheet at: Authorsonmission.com/resources.

Writing: How to craft the ultimate book introduction

The introduction is your first significant encounter with your reader. Think about it as an elevator pitch. To me, the introduction is the most important real estate of the entire book and, in fact, the most underutilized. Most authors underestimate the power to attract readers, inspire them to continue reading, and even gain subscribers and followers.

The introduction typically briefly explains what your book is about, its uniqueness, and what it can offer. It is also a great place to establish your credibility and why the reader should listen to *you*!

Remember that the book introduction also serves as a sales page, so it should be persuasive enough to give them a reason to purchase.

For example, if your book is published on Amazon, the "Read Sample" feature will help you sell your book. It provides potential readers with a glimpse of the first few pages, so you want to make sure that you touch every pain point, desire, goal, and solution that will be offered while keeping the reader engaged and, therefore, eager to continue reading.

Ideally, you want to create an instant connection, making it irresistible.

If your goal, or part of your "why," is to build an email list, you can offer a giveaway in the form of a checklist, a report, or a short ebook relevant to the book.

In exchange for the giveaway, your readers will opt-in via a landing page and enter their email addresses in a form.

Don't be surprised if people grab the giveaway without purchasing the book. But this can be a good thing because, even if you're not making a sale, you'll build your email list for the future, which we will discuss in Phase III.

The 5-Point Format for a Killer Introduction

1. Start by stating the problem.

80% of nonfiction readers turn to books to solve real-life problems. Be clear and straightforward with the issues that you are trying to solve with your book.

2. Present your ideas for a solution.

Most authors get this part wrong—they write the solutions to the problem they are trying to solve in the introduction. If you do that, your secrets are revealed way too early, and there's nothing more to anticipate.

It's like watching Taken when you know who kidnapped Liam Neeson's daughter. There's no suspense.

Instead, you must present the general idea or a broad approach at the start. Save the details for the meat of the book.

3. State the benefits to be gained from your book.

At this point, your reader is already thinking—*WIIFM? (What's In It For Me)*

Answer this question by painting a picture of a successful outcome from reading your book, maybe through an example or personal experience.

4. Show proof of credibility or expertise.

Share why and how your book answers your readers' problems and why they should believe you in the first place.

This could mean presenting your knowledge, experience, and expertise or showing tangible results from your research to back up the key ideas and solutions you are offering.

As the digital world expands, there are greater opportunities for artificial intelligence to be used to write content of all types and infuse your book with human qualities, and your audience will certainly appreciate it. They want to know who you are and what makes what you have to say valuable to them.

5. *End with a Call to Action. (Prompt them to read more.)*

Once you have established the case for your book, end the introduction, leaving the reader wanting more.

It should convey an intriguing promise coupled with a sense of urgency.

For example, in *The One Thing* by Gary Keller, the author concludes the introduction with a firm pronouncement of the promise and insight into the future: "*The One Thing* delivers extraordinary results in every area of your life—work, personal, family, and spiritual."

Who wouldn't want to keep reading with a call to action like that?

Crafting an introduction that enthralls, excites, and engages is critical to becoming a bestselling author. So, at this stage, I invite you to write a brief introduction, maybe 500 to 700 words. I guarantee it will get you in the right frame of mind for the next big milestone—working on the Rough Draft of your book.

Pro Tip: As I mentioned earlier, another benefit of the outline is that you can work on another section if you feel stuck. I feel the same way about the introduction. Often, much of what needs to be introduced at the beginning will come from the content you include in the manuscript.

So, don't stress about writing the introduction first. Many authors write the introduction near the end of the writing process.

Writing: How to write the book like a pro

Remember how I mentioned that I plowed through the writing process of my first book? Did you hear me say that it was actually good?

Thankfully, my then-girlfriend, now my wife, was good with academics, so she helped me take that first attempt to the next level with editing and proofreading. The point is that I had to start somewhere.

Know that your first draft may be poorly written, with much rambling, incomplete thoughts, and even disorganized content. And that is fine! This step aims to produce an initial draft from your book's first to the last chapter.

Staring at a blank page intimidates most aspiring authors so much that many of them never even get to start. Imagine how you will feel once you have an actual draft with real content in your hands! The feeling is actually quite surreal.

As I know too well, getting started is often the most challenging part. So many factors can deter someone from writing, but the simplest way I can suggest getting started is, as Nike's advertising campaign suggests, Just Do It.

In other words, get out of your head and into the grind of writing. If you really feel stuck, be sure to read the 11 hacks to overcoming writer's block and unlocking your creativity. I will share in just a moment.

In the meantime, let's look at the basic structure I use when writing each chapter.

1. Introduction - Some interesting things to use in the introduction to each chapter include an anecdote, examples, a quote, or a conversation. The idea is to keep the reader hooked and looking forward to the information you will share.
2. Main body - This is where you provide the meat and potatoes of the book. Are you offering a solution to a problem? Providing detailed information or relevant content? Be sure to include statistical data, evidence-based research, and examples, adding value to the reader and solidifying why they purchased your book.
3. Summary of the chapter - Similar to the conclusion, which we will talk about in the next section, provide the reader with a recap of the information you discussed. This is also a great place to include a call to action or exercises for the reader to implement what they learned.
4. Segue - Be sure to include a compelling transition, connecting the topic of discussion in one chapter with what the reader should anticipate in the next. Give them a hint of what they will learn by continuing to read, and you will keep them engaged and eager for more.

Pro Tip: Writing a book is a process, and you cannot expect perfection of yourself or the process. Whenever you get overwhelmed, frustrated, or facing writer's block, consider it just a part of the process to take breaks, find inspiration in a long walk in nature, and reset your energy. I guarantee you will return to your work feeling invigorated and energized, ready to tackle the next chapter or idea.

Writing: How to summarize the content with a well-written conclusion

The definition of a conclusion is the end of a process. Therefore, it is appropriate for the final pages of your manuscript to be called the conclusion.

Writing the book's conclusion aims to ensure your reader takes away and retains the key lessons from your book.

Think about it this way: Your reader has made it through the end of your book after a significant time investment. This is how to make your final message count.

You can maximize your profit by adding a call-to-action (CTA), using specific resources, links, and giveaways to help convert your readers into clients for your other services.

In your conclusion, provide your contact details, booking link, or website link.

Let's look at several tips for writing a conclusion that will interest your reader in learning more about you, possibly your services, and, more importantly, eager to read your next great book.

1. Start by recalling the hook of your book.

In the introduction, you set the stage for your book's promise. Now that the show is over, it's time to remind the reader of the rewards or values gained from reading your book.

2. Tie up loose ends with a quick summary.

Your readers might have already forgotten some of your key messages by the time they reach the end. Reinforce your key messages or ideas with a summary. You want to leave them with a clear understanding of this book before they move on to the next one.

3. Paint a bright future.

An unforgettable conclusion presents an ideal vision of the future as a result of practicing the lessons learned from reading your book.

4. Express gratitude.

Your readers stuck with you all the way to the end. Make sure to thank them sincerely.

5. End with a call-to-action.

Tell your readers what you want them to do after reading your book. This should not be a selling message but bring the ideas and concepts full circle, leaving them with marching orders or direction.
For example, in Brené Brown's book *Dare to Lead,* she concludes with the following: "Choose courage over comfort. Choose whole hearts over armor. And choose the great adventure of being brave and afraid. At the exact same time."

Lastly, this is the ideal place to ask for a review because, by the time they have reached the conclusion, they will have grasped the concept of your book and hopefully will want to share it with others.

Pro Tip: Ultimately, the conclusion is just as important as the introduction, so be sure to approach this chapter with the same care and intention as you did at the beginning of your book.

Writing: 11 Hacks to Defeat Writer's Block

We have all experienced it. That temporary condition when you stare at a blank screen, knowing that you have to get started, yet nothing comes to mind and you seemingly have nothing to say. Even the most prolific and renowned writers have experienced writer's block at some point. So don't worry if you find it difficult to get started.

Here is a list of hacks to help you overcome writer's block and get started on your writing journey.

1. *Work from your outline.*

Your outline is ordered sequentially, as we learned in Step 1, for two reasons.

The first is to guide you in writing your content in a logical way. The second is to help you stay on track and organized.

Complete your rough draft by sticking to your outline. Don't attempt to change it by moving things around or adding and deleting sections.

Save these tasks for later because finished is better than perfect at this point in the writing process.

2. *Get into the flow.*

Set aside all nagging thoughts like – *Will I find my voice? What is my writing style?* This sounds awful! – and trust the process.

These doubts will fade as you get into your writing flow.

3. *Use tech to help keep you organized and efficient and to deal with writer's block.*
Some of my favorite tools include:

- Scrivener - a management system for writing and organizing content
- Google Docs
- Voice In - Speech-to-Text Dictation - speech-to-text in real time
- ChatGPT - not recommended to write the entire manuscript but to generate ideas, titles, book descriptions, and even an outline
- Claude - similar to ChatGPT but can be used in certain situations
- Get Motivated Buddies - accountability partners
- Focusmate - another accountability system forcing you to focus on a specific task
- Freedom.to - helping you to focus your time and energy, enabling you to become more productive

4. *Establish a regular writing schedule.*

Getting your brain into the habit of writing starts with blocking off the same time every day to do it.

For example, write for two hours every morning from 8 am to 10 am. It does not matter where you are. Test and trial different things in the first week, and then find out what you are comfortable with, and then go with that flow.

It's important to note that just because it's your way, it doesn't necessarily mean it is the only way. You may find that you write better at 10 pm than at 10 am. You will not know until you try.

The point is to force yourself to commit to writing until your brain is so used to it that it becomes part of your daily routine, like working out at the gym.

5. *Set a daily writing target.*

How much work do you need to get done after every two-hour session? Is it writing 300 words or more?

Setting a specific target will help you work better, faster, and smarter each time. Start by setting a low target and increase it day by day as you get on with your progress.

By writing 300 words for two hours every day, you can get a book with 30,000 words or 150 pages, done in 100 days or roughly four months.

The goal is consistency.

6. *Stick to your deadline.*

Writers use the expression "write or die" – writing with desperation and urgency as if your life depended on it.

It's called a "deadline" for that reason.

Writers find that this mindset keeps procrastination at bay and drives them to accomplish their book goals on time. I am sure you have heard people say, "I have been working on a manuscript for ten years." While they may be okay with that timeline, the way I see it, you could have written dozens of books and completely changed your life in that time (or shorter)!

7. *Picture the final outcome.*

As you begin writing, you need to set a target length or a total word count for your book, as I alluded to in Step 1 when discussing the outline.

Are you working to finish a short eBook of 20,000 words or an epic showstopper of 100,000 words or more?

Below are the types of books categorized by length to give you an idea of the end product:

BOOK TYPE	NUMBER OF WORDS	READ TIME
Business White Paper	10,000	30 min. to 1 hour
Short eBook or Manifesto	20,000	1 - 2 hours
Short nonfiction book or novel	20,000 - 40,000	3 - 4 hours
RECOMMENDED – Standard nonfiction book or novel (200 - 400 pages)	50,000 - 80,000	4 - 6 hours
Long nonfiction book or novel	80,000 - 100,000	8 - 12 hours
Epic-length nonfiction or novel	100,000 +	12 hours +

8. *Resist the urge to edit.*

The trick to getting a lot of work done quickly is to keep writing and reserve judgment for later.

The number one reason some writers don't finish their book is that they edit and critique their work as they write. Get all the writing done as fast as you can. There will be plenty of time later to edit and fine-tune your work. And, of course, there is an entire step (Step 3) dedicated to the editing process.

Think of it this way: You are an ice sculptor with an idea for a beautiful piece in your head. You need to stack blocks of ice together before you start chipping away at it.

The same goes for your manuscript. You must stack the words and paragraphs together before you start chipping away at them.

9. Take a moment to appreciate your progress.

Read what you wrote yesterday to assess your work and to keep you in the mindset of getting more writing done.

Doing this will boost your confidence and motivate you to improve each time you write.

10. Take small breaks to avoid getting stuck.

Sometimes in the writing process, you hit a wall and words simply evade you.

Take a break from writing for a moment. Take a walk, a nap, or enjoy a little snack. Sometimes, a quick reboot is just what you need to get your brain back in the game.

11. Assign a writing buddy.

Writing is a painstaking, solitary endeavor and you will need a support system to make the process a little less difficult.

A writing buddy doesn't have to be a writer, but it can be helpful if you find someone who has written and published a book. Regardless of their author status, that person should be someone you trust who can keep you on track to accomplish your daily and weekly tasks.

If you are looking for someone to keep you motivated in the writing process, you can find a reliable partner with [GetMotivatedBuddies](). It's a matching platform to find people who can keep you accountable for your goals.

A buddy who understands your goals, listens to your struggles and boosts your confidence can bring out the best in you.

According to the [Association for Talent Development](), formerly the

American Society for Training and Development, you are 95% more likely to complete your goal with a buddy you meet with regularly than not having one at all.

So, to reach your writing goal faster, meet a writing buddy online by visiting getmotivatedbuddies.com.

Writing: Alternatives to writing the book yourself

Now, I understand that the title of this book is *How to Write a Bestseller,* implying that you will be the one writing it. Still, I would be doing you a disservice if I didn't acknowledge and explain the alternatives to actually putting words on paper yourself.

In fact, quite a few options are available to you if you doubt your abilities, don't have the time, or frankly don't want to do it yourself. And that is okay.

Within the following few pages, I will share information on the following:

- Ghostwriting
- Artificial Intelligence (i.e., ChatGPT)

Since I didn't have the financial resources to hire a ghostwriter to write my initial books, I had to write it myself. But now I am sure I will never write another myself. In fact, this book was also made possible because of one of our ghostwriters (angel writers).

Let's look at the ghostwriting process and how hiring a ghostwriter will allow you to focus on what you do best and give you a high-quality product that can easily make it to the top of the bestseller lists.

Ghostwriting Basics

Ghostwriting is a little-known secret that authors have been utilizing for years. In fact, some of the most popular books on the market were written by someone other than the author credited on the cover.

Let me give you some examples:

- The Pursuit of Happiness by Chris Gardner
- Onward by Howard Schultz
- The 360 Degree Leader by John C. Maxwell

While it is difficult to know how many books have been written by a ghostwriter, it is estimated that more than 60% of non-fiction books are ghostwritten.

Shocking right?

According to one recent survey, an estimated 4 million books are published yearly, whether through traditional or self-publishing methods. While there really is no way to know, I would guess that ghostwriters wrote a substantial percentage of those.

So, let's look at some of the benefits of hiring a ghostwriter to pen your book on your behalf:

1. Time-saving.

As I am sure you have figured out by now, writing a book is time-consuming. Of course, there are many reasons why you may think you don't have enough time to dedicate to it. For example, you already juggle a career and family and like to sleep. Or maybe you are looking to crank out your first book in a short period of time so you can begin earning income. No matter the reason you believe you do not have the time to put into the writing process, a ghostwriter will certainly be able to help.

2. Factors that are stopping you.

As we discussed earlier, you may have any number of things stopping you from writing a book. Although I can give you suggestions on how to overcome them, the reality is that it is okay to ask for help. In the writing arena, this help might come from someone writing the book for you.

3. Skills and experience.

Everyone has their own unique gifts and talents. Maybe you are not the most skilled writer and do not want to spend the time and energy to improve this skill. Why not hire someone who already possesses what it takes to create a manuscript without going through the learning curve yourself?

Just because hiring a ghostwriter is an option does not mean you are completely out of the loop unless you want to be. There are various types and levels of ghostwriting, which I want to share to prepare you for the next step, which is hiring a ghostwriter.

Of course, you must know what you want to write about to determine the type, skill, and experience level of a ghostwriter. Therefore, it would be helpful for you to have Step 1 of the writing process completed. If you have not already done so, I would go back and revisit Step 1, follow the checklists, and review the action items. This will help you to be better prepared to start the process and make it as streamlined as possible.

First things first, what type of book do you want to produce?

- Memoir/biography
- Business/leadership
- Self-help
- Inspiration/Motivation
- How-to

Knowing the niche and genre you want to publish in will help you select the ghostwriter with the most appropriate skill set and experience to help you.

Each ghostwriter will have their own experience and expertise in writing on a particular topic as well as the method they offer, so choosing a ghostwriter is not as simple as conducting a Google search and selecting the first one on the list.

While there are many questions that will help you select the right one and know if they are a good fit for *you* and *your* book writing project, let's take a look at a few:

1. Method of working with authors:

- Collaborative – You may want to provide all the content based on your experience and expertise through recorded interviews, previously written content, and research. The ghostwriter will compile it all and submit it to you for review. This may be a team effort to develop the title/subtitle, hook, and outline.
- Hybrid – You provide the ghostwriter with most of the elements of the ideation stage, including a well-defined outline, and collaborate only where anecdotes, stories, and examples may be necessary.
- Independent – You provide as much information to the ghostwriter as possible and allow them to create content as they see fit.

None of these methods is better or worse; it all depends on your comfort level of involvement, time, and the expense you are willing to commit to having a book written for you.

However, each ghostwriter may prefer how they are most comfortable working with authors, so you will need to discuss the method that will work best for both of you.

2. Experience level.

Just as diverse as the array of topics to write about, there is an equally diverse workforce of ghostwriters with those specific skills and experience.

While a ghostwriter may not necessarily have previous experience writing about your specific topic, they should have samples to demonstrate their own previous experience and capabilities.

A few things to consider:

- Is the work well organized and easy to read?
- Is there a consistent voice/tone throughout?
- Are you engaged and interested in reading it?

3. Availability, deliverables, and pricing.

The ghostwriting industry has taken off in recent years as more people are interested in writing a book. That also means a larger number of ghostwriters vying for the work.

Not only must the quality and experience meet your needs, but their services must also fit your expectations for timing, product, and, of course, budget.

The following are some additional questions to ask to ensure that you find a ghostwriter to suit your goal of producing a high-quality product that you can market, sell, and ultimately, return a profit for your investment.

As much as this is about writing a book, keep that last point in mind—you want to earn enough income to account for the expense you lay out for the ghostwriting process.

- Unless you are using a ghostwriting service, most independent ghostwriters manage multiple projects simultaneously. Do they have the capacity to write your book within your desired timeframe?

- Can the ghostwriter deliver content based on established milestones?
- What are the price, payment terms, and termination rights?
- Lastly, as a ghostwriter, they relinquish all rights to the content or from receiving credit for its publication. Is the ghostwriter willing to sign a non-disclosure agreement?

Pro Tip: Finding a ghostwriter with whom you click is important. There has to be a chemistry between and open communication to allow for feedback, revisions, and constructive criticism. Even though they are writing on your behalf, remember that this is your work of art and must be all you envision.

Pro Tip #2: The potential damage to your writing career before it even gets off the ground is enough reason to choose a ghostwriter appropriately. Remember that it is your name on the cover!

Where to Find a Ghostwriter

So, now that you understand what to look for in a ghostwriter, the next question is where to find them. Finding a ghostwriter can initially be as difficult as searching for any other service, such as a plumber, local painter, or auto repair shop.

The first place to go is the Internet. Doing a simple search on Google will undoubtedly open the door to a wide variety of ghostwriters worldwide, with varying experience levels and, of course, for every budget.

While this may be a place to start, many companies have sprung up over the years that serve as hubs or networking platforms to help you narrow down your search and connect with the right person. Some of these may include:

- Upwork
- Reedsy
- American Association of Ghostwriters
- To name a few…

I will caution you that while using one of the above platforms is certainly a great resource, proceed with caution. Each will help you narrow the search, but you must still do your due diligence to vet and qualify the *right* ghostwriter for your book writing needs.

Of course, if you are having trouble finding a ghostwriter to suit your needs, reach out to Authors on Mission, and we will connect you with an angel writer who best suits your needs.

Why are we so confident we can assist?

With a team of more than 450 angel writers in our circle, Authors on Mission is the only publishing company that allows you to pick your ghostwriter (or angel writer). All the other companies out there that provide ghostwriting services assign a ghostwriter to work with you, and you have to bear with them for 3, 6, or 12 months during the book-writing process. You won't believe it, but 90% of those companies don't even let you talk to your ghostwriter. Crazy! They will just ask you to come up with the outline, and then you will need to wait several months for your manuscript. Now, think about it. How on earth can that person, the ghostwriter, understand your ideas, message, story, vision, and experience? And how can they write your book in your style, with your unique personality? The truth is, they can't! Eventually, you'll figure out you've wasted your time, and then you think this entire ghostwriting is not for you, and then you try to write the book yourself. But sadly, most of the people who try to write the book themselves never finish it, their experience tainted by the process.

At Authors on Mission, we solve this problem! We know that THE most important thing for you is to produce a really high-quality book in your own authentic voice. And with our angel writers, we deliver that. But there's more! We will package it very professionally with a great cover and formatting, uplifting your brand, and then we'll publish and promote it to a guaranteed #1 bestseller spot in less than 6 months.

So go ahead and schedule a call with our author strategist to discuss your ghostwriting options: authorsonmission.com/call/

Artificial Intelligence

Last but not least, I will share with you an exciting method many authors use to guide them in creating their bestselling books: artificial intelligence (AI).

Technology is moving at the speed of light. Although the digital world may once again change when you are emotionally and psychologically ready to use it, the reality is that, soon enough, everything will become digital in some way, shape, or form.

So, why not take advantage of the help where we can? AI can help generate book ideas or help you get over writer's block if you are stuck. However, I will caution you that although tools such as ChatGPT can help in your writing process, there is no substitute for the human mind and all that it has to offer. Your stories, experiences, and expertise are priceless when creating original content, as only a human knows how.

That being said, I don't recommend using AI Tools to write your entire book, as Amazon can flag it as being plagiarized. You can certainly get inspiration from ChatGPT and get help coming up with titles, subtitles, and descriptions if you are stuck and need some examples or ideas. But I really recommend writing your manuscript on your own.

Key Takeaways: Step 2 – Writing

Although we have only concluded Step 2, you have tackled one of the hardest parts of becoming a bestselling author. Pat yourself on the back for getting this far. I am sure it was not easy, but I am so thankful you have stuck it out.

We covered a lot of content and I just want to summarize some of the things we discussed as we put the pieces together so that you can be sure you have completed each step of the process thus far:

- How to fast-track your research
- How to write the perfect book title and subtitle
- How to craft the ultimate book introduction
- How to write the book like a pro
- How to summarize the content with a well-written conclusion
- 11 hacks to defeat writer's block
- Alternatives to writing the book yourself

I mentioned that I did not want you to worry about grammar, spelling, or organization during the writing process. I simply wanted you to get the information out on paper. It is now time for us to look at how you will take your first draft, this first pass at a manuscript, and polish it like a jeweler polishes a diamond.

I assure you that you are well on your way to becoming a bestselling author. But if you have any questions or need extra support, please contact me at vikrant@authorsonmission.com.

STEP 3 – EDITING

Polishing the diamond to bring out its beauty

"In writing, you must kill your darlings."

—William Faulkner

Editing is the process of streamlining and refining the text so that the reader can get the most from your book.

The idea of having someone else review, pull apart, and change the document you worked so hard on may be intimidating and even offensive. In reality, a manuscript is a work that is best done with the help of others. If you open any book on the market, especially those published through traditional publishing methods, every acknowledgment page is filled with gratitude and appreciation to the editors for helping to bring the book alive. Ultimately, every bestselling book has (or should have) gone through multiple rounds of revisions and drafts.

I am not telling you that you must have an editor for your book to become a bestseller, but why not take every opportunity to position it the best you can? You are asking readers to take a chance on you; don't disappoint them with a manuscript full of typos and unclear thoughts. The bottom line is that this step can make the difference between a good book and a GREAT book!

Think about this scenario: you have been working on your manuscript for weeks, or maybe months, and have read it countless times. Those same words blend together, and your brain may even play tricks on you, making you believe there is a word where none exists or a comma where a period should be.

An editor serves as a fresh pair of eyes to catch, edit, and correct those things your eyes gloss over, not because you don't care about your work or the finished product, but because they are accustomed to seeing it.

Editors are trained and experienced at seeing things from a different perspective and improving upon them in several ways, which we'll talk about here in Step 3.

Remember, the goal is to create a product that will become a bestseller. It is not just the title, cover, or fancy font that propels it to the top of the charts. The content, of course, must be stellar, but ensuring that it is as polished as possible in all aspects is equally important.

So, what does polished mean? Putting your best foot forward, ensuring a clean, error-free, well-organized manuscript.

Some areas that an editor reviews and evaluates:

- Big-picture elements of the story or flow
- Identifying plot holes, weak character-building, confusing concepts, etc.
- Spelling, grammar, and punctuation
- Misused and/or missing words and improper phrasing
- Tone, style, and point of view

As the quote above by William Faulkner suggests, one aspect of the editing process is to eliminate some parts of your manuscript that you may be passionate about. They may hinder the reader's understanding of your book, be off-topic, or detour the reader too much.

While most writers oppose this idea, think of "killing your darlings" as serving the reader's interest ahead of yours as the writer, and you will be in the right frame of mind to edit.

In the following pages, I will shed light on the various types of editing and how to do each yourself, including:

- How to conduct a developmental edit: Checking the meat and potatoes
- How to line edit: Making sure every word counts
- How to copy edit: Ensuring accuracy and readability
- How to proofread: One last round for good measure
- How to hire an editor

I recommend editing the book yourself, but if this all seems like too much, or if you want to have your book reviewed by a professional editor, reach out at Authorsonmission.com. We have a team of editors who have worked on New York Times bestselling books and have the knowledge and expertise to take your book to the next level.

Editing: How To Conduct A Developmental Edit - Checking The Meat And Potatoes

Before you get down to taking words, sentences, and paragraphs apart, you need to assess the content. Review the meat and potatoes, so to speak, of the structure, flow, organization, and depth of the content.

The goal of this round is simply to make sure that all the essential information is in your book. You might consider this a "big picture" look.

Here are some questions to ask as you read the entire document from start to finish. Be sure to put yourself in the shoes of the reader. How would they read the manuscript and its takeaways?

- Does it have all the information I wanted to include in the outline?
- Is it organized, and does the flow make sense to the reader?
- Are the chapter titles, headers, or subheaders in the right place, and are they relevant to the content?
- Are there any inconsistencies or holes in the content that may leave the reader with more questions than answers?

Developmental editing does not focus on grammar, spelling, or any of the smaller details. During this step, you want to ensure that the broader elements of the content are well-developed and clear so the reader has an enjoyable experience with the content and will, therefore, provide positive feedback and, ultimately, refer it to others.

Pro Tip: Before you take on this step of editing, it is important to take a step back and separate yourself from the content, even taking some time away from it, to allow yourself to view it from a fresh perspective. You will be surprised at how you perceive something you have written once you distance yourself from the manuscript.

Editing: How to line edit - making sure every word counts

This is where you need to carefully pick your paragraphs, sentences, and words apart to make sure your writing is smart and accurate. It also ensures that you have written consistently in the same tone, voice, and style.

- Do the sentences flow well in every paragraph?
- Is each chapter introduced with a well-written paragraph?
- Does each paragraph prove the point you are trying to make?
- Are there too many points in this paragraph?
- Have you cut out unnecessary words, sentences, paragraphs, and sections?
- Could the same thought be expressed in fewer words or more clearly?
- Is the tense consistent throughout?
- And so on.

Line editing involves looking at every word closely and making it count towards the reader's understanding.

Here are a few quick and dirty tips to elevate your word choice or diction:

1. Watch out for homonyms.

The English language can be tricky, even if you are a native English speaker. Homonyms are words that sound the same but have different meanings. The wrong word will impact your reader's understanding of your work, and spell-check will not catch this; it requires a careful and skilled eye.

Examples:

- their/there/they're
- bare/bear
- allowed/aloud
- your/you're
- accept/except
- hear/here

2. *Be careful with synonyms.*

Before you whip out the thesaurus and replace your words with synonyms, make sure you know what the new word means. Look it up in the dictionary to make sure you're using it in the right context.

3. *Limit the use of jargon.*

Sometimes, technical terms get in the way of understanding what you're trying to say. Do you expect your audience to know technical jargon? If not, best to keep it simple.

4. *Cut out pretentious words and clichés.*

Aim for clarity and simplicity in your writing. Avoid using words like "sanguine" when you can write "cheerful" or "visage" instead of "face." The goal is to educate, not confuse. You also don't want to make the reader feel you are writing above their level of understanding. Your words should make them feel that you are speaking their language and that you understand their pain point, point of view, and perspective.

Pro Tip: While it is certainly possible to complete line editing yourself, this may be a great place to hire a professional to help you.

As explained earlier, you have probably read the manuscript so often that things like homonyms and jargon can easily be overlooked. And since you want to put your best foot forward, it is a good idea to identify a resource to help you achieve that.

Editing: How to copy edit - ensuring accuracy and readability

Copy editing is about the mechanics of each sentence. Typically, this is the final step before the last read-through or proofread.

During this process, the goal is to identify and correct any structural errors with sentences and individual words. This includes misplacement or missing commas, incorrect use of end punctuation, and incomplete sentences. You'd be surprised at how easy it is to end a sentence without finishing your thought!

Ultimately, the goal of copy editing is to ensure that your book is as error-free and polished as possible. This requires attention to detail and a keen knowledge of the rules of English and style.

Some things to look for include:
- Spelling – did you type you when *you* meant *your*, forgetting the last letter? Or did you mistakenly misspell the name of a quoted author?
- Grammar – For example, "The cart of groceries are already full" should be "The cart of groceries is already full."
- Punctuation - "After she ate one of the donuts, she realized that she should have bought a coffee too" – missing a comma after "donuts" and a period at the end.
- Spacing – do you have only one space instead of two between each sentence?
- Have you used certain words too frequently within a sentence or paragraph? For example, He lived in a big house with a big yard in the suburbs of a big city.
- Do the sentences go on forever without punctuation or maybe just a sentence fragment?

So, don't be scared if you are not familiar with the myriad rules of

English or the exact location and position for every comma. There are certainly professionals who can assist. Hang tight and I'll share how to find a professional editor shortly.

Pro Tip: Spell check is available in most, if not all, systems, including Microsoft Word and Google Docs. While it should not be used in place of the human eye, it is a great complement to help you catch those pesky errors that maybe you read over time and again but still have not caught.

Editing: How to proofread - one last round for good measure

Proofreading is the final step before Phase I of the process is complete. It requires rereading the manuscript and making final touches to ensure it is polished and ready for publishing.

So, what are you looking for when proofreading? While you were looking for "big picture" or high-level issues during the Developmental Editing stage, proofreading is quite the opposite—you are looking at the details, including mechanical inconsistencies such as typos, punctuation, spelling, and formatting mistakes.

To ensure your best opportunity to achieve bestselling author status, you must ensure that you have produced a book worthy of this status, which means reviewing it one final time with a fine-tuned comb.

What to look for when proofreading?

- Basic spelling and grammar
- Capitalization
- Verb tense
- Basic formatting

Pro Tip: *"In general, what is written must be easy to read and easy to speak; which is the same." — Aristotle*

If a paragraph doesn't make sense in your head, try reading it aloud and recording it using your phone. Playback your voice recording and ask yourself: Do the words roll off your tongue and make perfect sense? Or do they sound awkward, confusing, and contrived?

This is an easy way to test if you are articulating your ideas well. If a phrase or sentence sounds unclear and uncertain to you, you can be certain it will be just as unclear and uncertain to your reader.

Doesn't any gem appear more brilliant and valuable when polished to perfection? Why not complete every step of the editing process until you are satisfied with the result?

Of course, you will always find something in your book that can be better, and there will always be errors that will escape your attention. You have to be OK with not being perfect.

But the idea of Step 3 in the process is to ensure that you have done the due diligence necessary to present your product in the best possible light. You would not put out anything less than your best work in your personal life or career—why not wrap up the Produce Phase with pride in knowing that you have developed an idea, written the manuscript, and polished it, all to the best of your abilities.

The last thing I want to share with you about this step and as I have mentioned before, you do NOT have to rely solely on your own knowledge and experience to bring a polished product to fruition.

Let's briefly look at how you can hire an editor to help you at any stage of the editing process.

Editing: How to hire an editor

As you know, the writing process alone can be quite frustrating. For many authors, the thought of reviewing the content, pulling it apart, putting it back together, and reading it over and over again is more than they can handle.

So, as I alluded to throughout this step, help is available, and the process of finding an editor, or several editors for that matter, is not all that dissimilar to finding a ghostwriter as described previously. The avenues are the same.

What is different is understanding exactly what you are hiring for. Now you are familiar with the various types of editing and the function of each, let's review some basic questions to help you identify an editor who will suit your needs.

Also, like ghostwriters, not all editors are equal, and some may specialize in type or style or may have more experience in a particular niche or genre. Be sure to ask the right questions to ensure the right fit.

- What type of editing does the professional offer/specialty?
- What niche or genre do they have experience in?
- Do they have the availability to manage your project within your timeline?
- What is the cost of their services?

While all of the questions are relevant to accomplishing the task, it is critical to understand the factors contributing to pricing at each level to determine your budget and whether an editor fits within it.

How Editors Price Their Services

Whether you are looking for developmental, copy or line editing, or proofreading, pricing depends on several factors, such as:

- Stage (s) of editing required (i.e., developmental, line, copy editing, or proofreading)
- The complexity. Scholarly writing with multi-layered notes and ideas will cost more.
- The deadline. The tighter the deadline, the higher the cost.
- Your writing experience. Making bad writing better is more demanding work and costs more.
- Page count or word count. The more content the editor needs to cover, the more it will cost.

Let's look at an example of what a copy editor may charge for their services.

An experienced copy editor will charge between $0.05 to $0.10 per word for nonfiction, business, or self-help books. For example, if your book is 50,000 words, the cost is around $2,500 to $5,000, depending on the quality of the writing and the deadline.

Finding the right copy editor is a time-consuming, rigorous process but well worth the expense to help polish your diamond to a shine.

The cost of proofreading services also depends on the lead time or deadline and the book's length. But it is not as expensive as copy editing. Proofreaders charge around $0.025 per word for a nonfiction book. For example, if your book's length is 50,000 words, then proofreading will cost you around $1,250.

The value of what an experienced professional editor brings to your manuscript cannot be understated. So, while I am not staking the claim that you MUST use the services of an editor, utilizing an editor for one, if not all, of these functions is highly recommended to help you position your book for bestseller status. Don't forget that my team and I at Authorsonmission.com can connect you with an editor if you want to go that route.

Pro Tip: No matter the stage or level of editing required, it is a standard industry practice that the document be marked/edited using Track Changes and Comments in Microsoft Word and the Suggesting function in Google Docs so that you can see and accept all changes and suggestions. Although they are professionals, you, as the author, have the final say in accepting or rejecting each recommendation.

Key Takeaways: Step 3 – Editing

You now have a fully edited, polished manuscript ready for the next Phase – Publishing! You should be very proud of yourself and your accomplishments at this point.

But we are not done yet!

Before we move on to Phase II, let's review all that we learned in Step 3:

- How to conduct a developmental edit: Checking the meat and potatoes
- How to line edit: Making sure every word counts
- How to copy edit: Ensuring accuracy and readability
- How to proofread: One last round for good measure
- How to hire an editor

I want to remind you that you are not alone on this journey to becoming a bestselling author. You can always contact me with any questions or a little reassurance when the going gets tough at vikrant@authorsonmission.com.

PHASE II – PUBLISH

How to package, publish, and distribute your book in 3 simple steps

Before the internet, the only way to get published was to get your book on a bookstore shelf, which meant connecting with a literary agent and getting picked up through traditional publishing methods.

And it was this almost impossible pipe dream that only the most powerful and connected authors could crack.

And while that industry is certainly still alive and well, it's not the only dog in the game anymore.

To be successful, you will need to navigate through the Amazon self-publishing arena, where 90% of the books in the global market are now sold.

In Phase II of the 1-page Bestseller Checklist, we will be:

1. Adding the important elements that will make your book saleable, such as book description and cover design
2. Creating a pleasurable reading experience on Kindle and Paperback – Book Design
3. Getting your book into the hands of your readers –
4. Publishing and Distribution

Let's take a look at the three-phase system again and see where we are:

You can download a printable version of the "1-page Bestseller Checklist" at <u>Authorsonmission.com/resources</u>.

I will walk you through how to become a bestselling author, including positioning, design, and, ultimately, distribution!

Are you ready to move on to this next very important part of the journey?

Don't worry—I'll be right here with you.

STEP 4 – POSITIONING

Positioning your manuscript to make it irresistible

Writing a good book is essential, but positioning it to fly off the shelves is another. If you want readers to enjoy your book, it must have the vital elements that will draw them in and make them want to start reading.

These elements may not be directly related to your book's idea, but positioning your book well conveys a powerful message about its value.

In Step 4, you'll learn about the essential elements that will exhibit the uniqueness and legitimacy of your book, attract readers, and have them eager to share it with their friends.

- How to create a book description to increase book sales
- How to write an acknowledgment to win hearts
- How to write an author bio
- How to choose your Author picture
- How to assign an ISBN to your book

You have made it this far. Nothing is holding you back from completing these next steps other than your own self-doubt or limiting beliefs. Continue following along with me as I take you step-by-step closer toward having a finished product in your hand, ready to be published.

Positioning: How to create a book description to increase book sales

According to a recent study, nearly 4 million new book titles are published each year in the US alone, including self-published authors. That's certainly many titles readers have to sift through to find yours.

While crafting the right title and subtitle are critical to being discovered, think about what other factors will contribute to readers finding and, more importantly, buying your book.

Consider this scene: a potential reader scrolls through title after title on their Amazon account, reading each description carefully to pick their next read. They arrive at yours, and although the title initially caught their attention, they are captivated by the insight you have provided them with in just a few short paragraphs. They click ADD TO CART, and off they go, eager to receive your book on their digital device or at their door. Boom! Just like that, you have captured a new reader simply by crafting a well-thought-out, well-written description.

Here are some recommendations for making your book description stand out from the crowd, getting you the attention and new readers you desire.

To stand out in the competitive Amazon market, a clever book description will make sure that your potential reader knows:

1. Your book exists.
2. Your book is actually good and is worth their time and money.
3. You are a credible author and expert.
4. Your writing is serious, thoughtful, and professional.

Ideally, your book description should be so engaging that it convinces your target reader to do the following on your Amazon page:

1. "Read more" of the description and reviews.
2. "Look inside" the sample pages of your book.
3. Click "Buy"

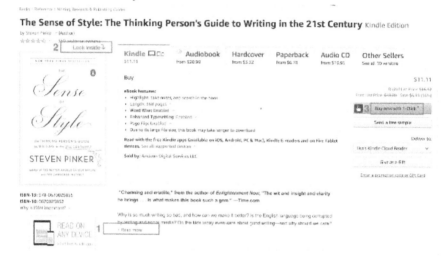

So, let's look at some recommended strategies for writing a killer book description:

1. ***Write an enticing opening sentence.***

If you've captured your potential buyer's attention with a great title and an amazing book cover, your next step is to lure the target to "read more" with an enticing opening sentence.

It's important to be specific yet brief, to say a lot without saying too much.

You must apply some clever copywriting strategies to craft a well-written first sentence.

Here are a few examples of great opening sentences of books about writing:

Example 1: Lure with curiosity.

"*Why is so much writing so bad, and how can we make it better? Is the English language being corrupted by texting and social media? Do the kids today even care about good writing? — and why should we care?*" – (Sense of Style by Steven Pinker)

Example 2: Open with a problem you aim to solve.

Whether you're writing a rags-to-riches tell-all memoir or literary journalism, telling true stories well is hard work. In "You Can't Make This Stuff Up," Lee Gutkind, the go-to expert for all things creative nonfiction, offers his unvarnished wisdom to help you craft the best writing possible. - (You Can't Make This Stuff Up by Steven Pinker)

Example 3: Charm with a personal story.

Advice on writing and on life from an acclaimed bestselling author: "Thirty years ago, my older brother, who was ten years old at the time, was trying to get a report on birds written that he'd had three months to write. It was due the next day. We were out at our family cabin in Bolinas, and he was at the kitchen table close to tears, surrounded by binder paper and pencils and unopened books on birds, immobilized by the hugeness of the task ahead. Then my father sat down beside him, put his arm around my brother's shoulder, and said, 'Bird by bird, buddy. Just take it bird by bird.'" - (Bird by Bird: Some Instructions on Writing and Life by Anne Lamont)

2. *Use your keywords.*

Writing a successful book description means strategically using your keywords to improve your book's searchability. If you recall, we discussed keywords early in the book when we discussed finding a topic. Keywords, specifically finding profitable keywords, will come up again in Step 6.

This is a clever way of seamlessly getting those keywords in your description in ways that sound natural and effortless, as opposed to pushy and contrived. But there is no need to fill the description with keywords if it means it will be an indecipherable mess.

Pro Tip: Never sacrifice readability over keyword optimization.

3. *Use bold and italic words or phrases.*

Emphasizing words or phrases with bold or italics should be done sparingly.

Use this formatting technique to highlight your book's best features, the problem you're solving, or the solution itself.

Check out the effective use of bold and italics in the book description for The Heart to Start: Stop Procrastinating & Start Creating.

4. *Replace text blocks with multiple paragraphs.*

An effective paragraph only has three sentences: a topic sentence, an explanation, and a conclusion.

If it's longer than that, you risk losing your reader's attention.

Consider breaking huge text blocks into shorter paragraphs to improve readability.

Turning Pro: Tap Your Inner Power And Create Your Life's Work has a great example of chopping up the book description into short lines of brilliant copy.

5. *Use bullets or lists.*

The purpose of your book description on Amazon is to sell your book.

Think of it as your storefront in a busy and crowded digital marketplace.

And when you only have a few seconds to hold a buyer's attention, you must quickly lay out your value proposition in a list form.

Read the description for The Elements of Style that details the updates on the 100-year-old classic in a short list.

6. *Use blurbs or reviews.*

If your book has earned a glowing review from a credible source, put it at the front and center of your book's description.

Consider how often you buy a product or service because of a recommendation from a friend or a positive review online.

In the book description of Sense of Style, the review from *Time* is used as a headline.

7. *Mention awards and notable achievements.*

The opening sentences of your book description (approx. 300 characters) are prime real estate. Amazon cuts the paragraph beyond the first four lines of text.

So, you need to be strategic about the order of your description by leading with the accolades to entice the buyer to hit "Read more."

The book description for Bad Blood: Secrets and Lies in a Silicon Valley Startup is a good example of leading with praise and awards and saving the actual premise of the book for last.

8. *Wrap it up nicely.*

As with any kind of writing, your short book description must have a strong ending.

Consider the following compelling description enders designed to convert or close a sale.

Example 1: End with a call-to-action.

Take your first step and click the buy button. Download The Heart to Start, *and unlock your inner creative genius today!*

Example 2: End with a takeaway.

Offering new ways of understanding the genre, this practical guidebook will help you thoroughly expand and stylize your work.

Example 3: End with a vision for success.

What we get when we Turn Pro *is we find our power. We find our will and our voice and we find our self-respect. We become who we always were but had, until then, been afraid to embrace and live out.*

9. ***Invite prospects to connect on social media or your website.***

A quick mention of your social media handle or website in your description lets the prospect know you are open to connecting.

Take this opportunity to gain followers, build an audience, and gain trust.

10. ***Bonus: Analyze how your book description compares with your competition.***

To find competitors in the same book category, check out the titles under the section "Customers Also Bought …" Go through each title suggestion and see how your book description compares.

What strategies have they applied? What is the readers' feedback like?

Use this intel and feed it into your marketing strategy to sell more books.

I also want to add that although I do not recommend writing the entire manuscript using ChatGPT, it can certainly be useful in writing an amazing, eye-catching book description that will attract readers and compel them to add your book title to their cart.

Here's the prompt you can use in Chat GPT to create an amazing book.

My book title is _____

And my book's table of contents is:
-
-
-

Please write a compelling Amazon description with proper formatting and bullet points with a call to action to get the book.

Pro Tip: As you complete the book description, ask yourself, "Why would I read this book?" If you can answer sincerely and believe your response, you have accomplished your goal of crafting a well-written book description.

Positioning: How to write an acknowledgment to win hearts

The Acknowledgments section is where you express your gratitude and appreciation for the people who helped you with your book.

It's a special space to give thanks and recognition publicly and permanently.

You can thank anyone who you feel contributed to your book significantly. For example:

1. Family members (spouse, children, parents)
2. Friends
3. Editors/people who worked on the book production
4. Publishers
5. Coworkers/assistants
6. Agents/managers
7. Contributors/advisors/sources of information
8. Teachers/mentors/bosses
9. Personal heroes/Inspirations

Keep it short, around 300 words, and make it sincere.

Below is a straightforward message of appreciation from author Joanna Penn:

Acknowledgements

Dedicated, with thanks, to all those writers who have impacted my life with their non-fiction books.

Thank you to my audience at The Creative Penn. Your support enables me to continue the journey of being a creative entrepreneur.

Thanks to everyone who completed my survey about writing non-fiction. Special thanks to those quoted in the book: Dr Karen Wyatt, Leeza Baric, and Ali Luke.

Thanks to Jane Dixon Smith at JD Smith Design for the book cover and interior print design, to Liz Dexter at LibroEditing for proofreading, and to Alexandra Amor for beta reading and double-checking attributions.

Guy Kawasaki's book acknowledgment is warm and friendly. The hyperlinks to the social handles of select people are a nice touch.

Acknowledgments

In giving advice, seek to help, not please, your friend.
—Solon

VERSION 2.0

My thanks to the readers of my drafts. They suggested hundreds of changes that made the book more relevant and useful. Ankit Agarwal, Biji Anchery, Christopher Batts, Mark Bavisotto, Stephen Brand, Dr. Julie Connor, Gergely Csapó, David Eyes, David Giacomini, Oskar Glauser, Allan Isfan, David F. Leopold, Eligio Merino, David Newberger, Greta Newborn, Mike Sax, Derek Sivers, Dale Sizemore, Eleanor Starr, Steven Stralser, Leslie Tiongco, Julius Vincze, and Maruf Yusupov.

Special thanks to these folks, who went above and beyond the call of duty: Raymond Camden, Mark Coopersmith, Andy Dahlen, Peg Fitzpatrick, Michael Hall, Chelsea Hunersen, Mohanjit Jolly, Bill Joos, Doug Leone, Bill Reichert, Beryl Reid, Peter Relan, Mike Scanlin, Ian Sobieski, Stacy Teet, and Hung Tran.

My gratitude to the Portfolio team: Rick Kot, Will Weisser, Adrian Zackheim, Diego Núñez, Stefanie Rosenblum, Victoria Miller, and Tara Gilbride. It's good to work with the A Team again. It's good to be working with you guys again. I hope I didn't drive you too crazy.

Positioning: How to write an author bio to showcase your expertise

In the Book Description, we've talked about how you can convince your target readers why they should buy your book.

In this section, we'll talk about why they should read what you have written and what qualifies you to be the one to share it.

It's your dedicated space where you can tell the story of the pen (you) who wrote on the paper (your book).

Getting your "Author Bio" section right will influence book sales and media attention, increasing the chances of your book becoming a success.

"Author reputation" is a major factor determining book buying.

Readers will carefully scrutinize the details in your author bio more than your book. After all, they are about to invest significant time and money in YOU as the author. You should put your best foot forward to demonstrate that you are the right choice.

How to write your author bio:

1. Present your credentials as an authority on your book's subject. Make a case for why the reader should listen to what you have to say, but be careful not to overstate it.

2. Highlight your significant achievements to help your reader understand why you are an authority on your book's subject.

3. Include the books you've written. If this is your first book, highlight any previously widely published work and your website. Carefully name-drop a VIP. But remember, you are hitching your wagon on someone else's good name, so make sure your connection is true.

4. Keep it short and interesting, ideally under 200 words.

Pro Tip: Research your competitors' books and look for their author bios. Take note of the sequence and manner of how they have written their bios.

The author bio is another component of positioning your book where you can benefit from ChatGPT's efficiencies. Include your biographical details in the prompt and ask the AI to craft a bio like a competitor's.

ACTION ITEMS:

Using the template on the left column, complete your author bio on the right column.

1. Statement to establish credibility on the subject	
2. Mention previous written work or past achievements	
3. Endorsement from a VIP, an institution, or an award-giving body	
4. Include some personal information	
5. Link to your website	

You can download a printable version of this Action Sheet at Authorsonmission.com/resources.

Positioning: How to Choose Your Author Picture to Gain Trust

A picture is worth a thousand words, and so is your Author Photo.

This is the official photo that appears on the back of your book cover, Amazon Author page, Author website, About the Author, and social media platforms.

Choosing your favorite photo from Facebook or your high-quality wedding photo as your Author Photo can be tempting. But choosing an Author Photo is something that you need to sit down and really think about.

Selecting the wrong photo can send a negative signal to your readers. There are two main ideas that your Author Photo should convey:

1. The kind of books that you write

If you're writing thriller novels, you don't have to show your colorful, cupcake-loving side.

Instead, a serious pose in black and white will show your readers that you are writing something dark and mysterious.

Your Author Photo will inform readers about your writing style, tone, and genre. It gives them the impression of what kind of book you have in store for them.

2. Your authority

Your Author Photo has the power to convey a message to your readers.It can suggest how well you know a specific subject and be used to build trust among your potential readers.

Based on that picture, readers can also sense whether you're a professional or an amateur. If your Author photo shows you making a wacky face, no one will take you seriously unless you're writing a book about jokes.

Will you be perceived as the go-to person for that topic when they see your Author Photo?

Or will you be perceived as someone who is just pretending?

Determine what message you want to convey by carefully planning your Author Photo.

There are no hard and fast rules on what makes a good Author Photo. It all depends on how you want to be perceived. Generally, you would want to present your best self, and having a professional photographer with a solid portfolio in headshot photography might be the best to help you achieve that.

Pro Tip: Try doing an A/B test (split test) with your friends, family, and target readers, providing them with two pictures and asking them to tell you which resonates with them.

Positioning: How to Assign an ISBN to Your Book

An International Standard Book Number (ISBN) is a 13-digit product identifier for a printed book, audiobook, eBook, or video used by publishers, booksellers, libraries, internet retailers, and other supply chain participants for ordering, listing, sales records, and stock control purposes.

What is an ISBN for?

The ISBN aims to establish and identify one title or edition of a title in a specific format from one specific publisher.

Where do you get an ISBN?

The U.S. ISBN Agency at Bowker is the only official source of ISBNs in the United States and its territories.

With an ISBN, you can manufacture and sell your publications anywhere in the world.

The U.S. ISBN Agency can only assign ISBNs to publishers located in the United States and its territories. Publishers in other countries must obtain their ISBNs from their local ISBN agency.

Do you need one?

If you publish exclusively on Amazon, the quick answer is NO; you don't need an ISBN. eBooks don't require one; only printed books do.

If you opt to publish a paperback exclusively on Amazon, it will assign your printed book an ISBN for free. Should you get an ISBN for your book anyway?

Probably. Any publisher intending to sell books or book-like products in physical bookstores, wholesalers, or other online stores needs an ISBN.

How do you get an ISBN?

You get an ISBN by purchasing it online on Bowker Identifier Services. The process is easy and self-explanatory on the site.

How much does an ISBN cost?

Source: Bowker Identifier Services

Key Takeaways: Step 4 - Positioning

Ultimately, positioning is about creating a space for your book in the reader's mind, and how they perceive it can help, inspire, or engage them.

A well-positioned book will help you achieve your goal of becoming a bestselling author, ensuring you meet your target reader's objectives.

- How to create a book description to increase book sales
- How to write an acknowledgment to win hearts
- How to write an author bio
- How to choose your Author picture
- How to assign an ISBN to your book

Some of these tasks in this step may seem foreign, especially if this is your first book. I can assure you that I was right where you are now, and after having written and reviewed my share of book descriptions, acknowledgments, and author bios, I have seen everything imaginable. I am here to help you become a bestselling author, so I will not steer you wrong. Reach out at vikrant@authorsonmission.com.

STEP 5 – DESIGN

Creating a great-looking book

Book Design is an often-overlooked part of the publishing process. After all, they say you can't judge a book by its cover. But of course, we all do.

Book design is not only what your book looks like on the outside. It sends a message about how it looks on the inside as well. When you publish your book on Amazon, you are publishing your book and, more importantly, your brand. People will judge you, your programs, the services you offer, and your company based on the quality of how your book looks. So, I cannot stress enough the importance of this section on design.

In fact, design is one of the trickiest parts of self-publishing.

Whether you decide to go at it by yourself or hire a professional to do it for you, you'll need to know what to look out for.

It's best to have a basic idea of what works and what doesn't so you at least know what to ask for or what to do yourself.

In this section, we'll be going through the basics up to the advanced book design techniques, including:

- How to Design your Kindle book cover to sell
- How to make a Paperback Cover that will stand the test of time
- How to format your ebook to keep your readers engaged

- How to design a captivating Paperback layout
- How to design your author website to establish your authority

I highly recommend hiring experts for your cover design and book formatting to ensure you create a quality product that will sell and be recommended to other readers. If you have some funds and are really serious about your book, hire a professional. Don't try to do this yourself, although, in the following few pages, I will explain how you can do it yourself if you choose to.

Professional designers have done this thousands of times and will know what will look best to attract your target reader. If you need some help identifying the designer who will be best suited to help you with your particular book project, be sure to reach out to us at Authorsonmission.com, where we have a team of seasoned book cover designers, many of whom have created New York Times bestselling book covers.

Although you may hire a professional, I still recommend reading the upcoming pages on how to do it yourself. You will get an idea of what to expect from your book cover designer and formatter.

In this section, I will share tips and tricks to create attention-grabbing covers and interiors that reflect the book's topic, genre, and tone and, most importantly, draw the reader in to want to buy and read it, which I will cover here in Step 5.

Design: How to design your Kindle book cover to sell

In the digital world, where people are inundated with content, images, and videos, they quickly scan headlines and graphics, searching for information in the fastest time possible amidst all the competition.

This means your Kindle book cover needs to be given a lot of thought to grab your target reader's attention quickly.

This chapter will discuss how to design your Kindle book cover, choosing between the DIY approach or outsourcing a professional book designer.

Creative Strategies for Designing Nonfiction Book Covers

Nonfiction readers need to immediately understand what your book is about just by looking at the cover.

The title must convey the premise prominently to help them decide if the book is for them. That is why most nonfiction titles are extra-long and require a talented designer to transform that content into a visually appealing cover.

Consider the lengths of these bestselling nonfiction book titles:

- Bad Blood - Secrets and Lies in a Silicon Valley Startup (10 words)

- The Life-Changing Magic of Tidying Up -The Japanese Art of Decluttering and Organizing (14 words)

- The Subtle Art of Not Giving a F*ck - A Counterintuitive Approach to Living a Good Life (17 words)

- The Coddling of the American Mind - How Good Intentions and Bad Ideas are Setting Up a Generation for Failure (19 words)

Below are five creative strategies designers use to present all that content in a stunning book cover and sell lots of copies.

Strategy 1:
Beautiful Single Photo Layout

This is a brilliant image choice to pique your interest in a nerdy subject.

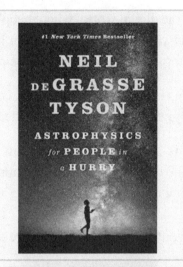

Strategy 2:
Big and Bold Typography

It's hard to ignore this book when the title is designed to punch you in the face.

Strategy 3:
Elegant Minimalism

Tiny typeset letters on a clean backdrop are all this book needs to stand out.

Strategy 4:
Striking Contrast

There's nothing subtle about the bold black lettering on a color that screams for attention.

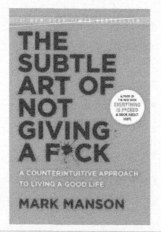

Strategy 5:
Clever Illustration

The drawn image of grads in a "failed" assembly line is a clever visual cue to read the extra-long title.

Five Steps to DIY an eBook Cover Design

Keeping these strategies and your visual skill level in mind, here are the DIY steps to bringing a book cover to life with great design.

1. Curate Design Inspirations

Put together a collection of book cover designs that inspire you on Pinterest. Keep an eye out for book covers in your genre on Amazon and assess how your book cover design can stand out.

2. Select and Download Image Assets

Here are FREE image sources you can use in exchange for artist credit. Check each site for attribution guidelines.

- Flickr
- Pixabay
- Pexels
- Free Images
- Unsplash
- Wikimedia Commons

PAID image sources:

- Depositphotos
- Stock unlimited
- Shutterstock

3. Set Kindle eBook Cover Dimensions

File Format	JPEG or TIFF
Ideal Cover Size	2,560 x 1,600 pixels
Ideal ratio	1.6:1

4. Design Two Cover Art Versions on CANVA

Canva Book Covers is a free web-based graphic design app where you can select and upload images, use templates, and create layouts.

If you can design slides on PowerPoint, you can easily work with Canva as it has a similar interface.

See these beautiful cover designs made using the Canva workspace:

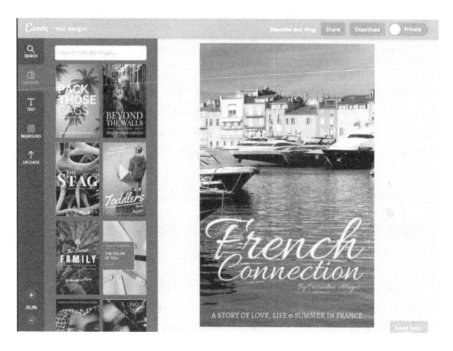

5. Get started with Canva by watching this tutorial. A/B Test Book Cover Designs Using **pickfu**

Upload your two book cover art designs and run a poll on pickfu to see what works best. Here's an example:

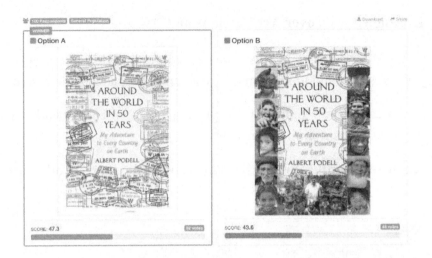

Pro Tip: If you sell on Amazon, make sure your book cover design pops. Don't go with a white background because Amazon uses a white background, too. Use bright and contrasting colors like yellow, red, or black to make your book stand out.

Five Steps to OUTSOURCING eBook Cover Design

Everyone is good at judging books by their covers, but not everyone is a good book cover designer.

If you do not have design skills and cannot design the book cover yourself, it is best to hire a professional with years of experience. Finding a designer that meets your needs is similar to the steps for finding a ghostwriter or editor.

1. Find a professional graphic designer through various marketplaces. Choose from a list of platforms here on our resource page: Authorsonmission.com/resources.
2. Brief the artist about your book using the description and your Pinterest book cover inspirations.
3. Agree with the artist on the scope of work, cost, and deadline.
4. Receive at least two versions of the final book cover designs.

5. A/B test the book cover designs using pickfu.

Pro Tip: An eBook cover should give the reader a sneak look at what they should expect in the book so as you design or project the scope to the designer, keep in mind how you want the book to be perceived, including the subject matter and tone.

Design: How to make a Paperback cover that will stand the test of time

Once you finish the Kindle cover, it's time to get your Paperback book cover ready.

A physical book will never go out of style, no matter how much futurists say it will. It's important to note how your book will not only stand out but also stand the test of time.

While the basics of cover design that I shared for creating the eBook cover still apply, there are a couple more elements that are unique for a printed book:

The Spine

If your book isn't featured prominently on a bookshelf, chances are it will be displayed with other books with only the spine facing out, which means that tiny piece of literary real estate is your only chance of grabbing someone's attention.

Make sure that your book's identity is clearly conveyed on the spine.

Along with your book's title logo, subtitle, and author name, the art from the cover must flow along the spine, but not in a way that crowds or takes away from the text.

The title should always be what's most prominent.

The Back Cover

If your front cover strikes the interest of a potential reader, chances are they'll pick it up, turn it over, and start reading the back. That's when you've raised the chances of your book being purchased, so it is critical that you make a great impression with the back cover.

Make sure your artwork flows from the cover to the back. You don't want a jarring difference between styles.

Write a clear yet attention-grabbing back cover synopsis.

You should be able to convey your book's message in about 200 words or less using short, breezy paragraphs, just enough to get potential readers curious.

So, what does all that mean?

Here are a few tips for writing your back cover description:

- Remember that you are trying to get the reader to purchase the book so be sure to grab their attention by providing a brief outline of what they should expect to find.

- Use short paragraphs or even bullet points.

- Speak directly to what you will offer the reader. For example, maybe you are solving a problem. End with a direct promise or perhaps even ask the reader a question.

Pro Tip: This back cover description should not be a summary of the book but a quick, almost salesy pitch to engage the reader and entice them to want to learn more about what you have to say.

Creating your Paperback Cover on Amazon Kindle

KDP (Kindle Direct Publishing) templates make it easy to create a print-ready paperback cover with programs that can open a PNG or PDF. Download a cover template.

Here is Kindle's guide to setting up your back-cover design using their template:

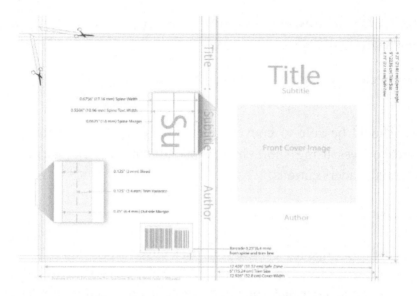

After applying these specs, take a look at the final paperback cover our designers created for one of our clients:

It's easy to bring your cover ideas to life using free web tools and templates in KDP and Canva.

If the thought of designing your book cover gives you pause, you can hire an expert to do it for you. I recommend following the steps I outlined previously in the ghostwriting section in Step 2.

Be sure to find a book cover designer who will capture your book theme and translate it into art. We have listed some places where you can find the best cover designers on our resource pages. Check it out here: Authorsonmission.com/resources.

Also, note that if you are hiring a cover designer, the same designer can do both your Kindle and paperback covers and audiobooks if needed.

Pro Tip: The idea behind your eBook and paperback covers is to grab the reader's attention and steal it away from the myriad of other books, videos, podcasts, and movies vying for their attention.

While it may be tempting to design the cover to be startling, outlandish, or thrilling, and therefore, eye-catching, remember that it must also give the reader a sense of what your book is about.

Design: How to format your eBook to keep your readers engaged

Although the cover of your book is what entices viewers at the beginning, what's inside will keep them interested. How your book looks and reads may be what keeps the reader reading or forces them to put it down.

Laying out the inside pages of your book is critical to your success as an author—the key being readability! Again, if you have some funds and are really serious about your book, my first preference would be to hire a professional book formatter instead of doing it yourself. But in the next few pages, I will explain how to do it yourself if you want to.

So, what is formatting exactly? While the process is different in both eBook and Paperback formats, the elements will be the same and include:

- Font size and type
- Page numbering (not included in eBook)
- Line and paragraph spacing
- Margins and headers/footers (only relevant in Paperback books)

In other words, all of those things will help to produce a visually appealing book.

Pro Tip: You don't want to turn people off by presenting them with a headache-inducing format with fonts that are too big and bold or, conversely, too small to read. You want to ensure consistency in all styles, symmetry in margins and spacing, and page numbering that is easy to understand.

Kindle has developed online tools such as Kindle Create to make it easy for self-publishers.

Use Kindle Create to create a "reflowable" or Print Replica Kindle Package Format (KPF) file.

Reflowable eBooks allow for a smooth digital reading experience. It lets the reader resize text on all Kindle devices, including tablets, phones, and e-readers.

How can you make your manuscript "reflowable"?

As the saying goes, "There is an app for that." One such tool is Atticus, which makes formatting your manuscript quick and easy. Just upload your Word document into the app, select your preferences for the style and feel, and instantly create beautifully formatted eBooks and print books.

Of course, hiring a professional to format your Kindle book for you is also an option. You can find a list of formatters on our resource list or reach out to Authorsonmission.com, and we will be happy to connect you with a professional we have worked with on any of our New York Times bestselling books.

Design: How to design a captivating Paperback layout

The permanence of printed books demands perfection in typesetting and formatting.

While I don't want to tell you there are particular standards to abide by or guidelines to follow, the goal is that you want your reader to enjoy the experience from start to finish. A well-executed book interior has great flow and a modern layout that reads pleasantly; the line spacing is on-point, the margins let the paragraphs breathe, and the words are where they should be.

Think about the last book you read. What did you enjoy about the visual presentation of the book? Were the line spacing and font size conducive to reading? If there were images or diagrams, were they placed strategically to optimize their visibility? What about the margins—was there too much white space, or was each page crowded with words?

Of course, you will never please everyone, and although most readers might find it very appropriate to the eye, someone will always have something to say. You are not writing this book for the naysayers, and I guarantee there will always be some, so go ahead and create a way.

Unfortunately, most writers forget the importance of the design principles for interior pages, resulting in a poor reading experience. You might end up getting bad reviews just because of the poor interior design.

Enhance the reading experience with these six important elements of a paperback layout.

1. Margins

These are the blank areas that surround the text on every page. The page margin includes the top, bottom, left, right, gutter, inner, and outer margin.

The gutter margin is the area used for the binding process. It is on the very inside of both pages.

In the top margin or header, you can add text about the book name, chapter name, and page number. This text is called the running head.

The bottom margin or the footer is where you will usually see the page number. The placement of the page number is at your discretion, with no particular rules or standards.

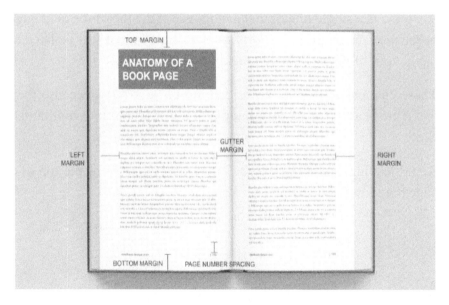

Another important part of the book page is the bleed, which goes beyond the page margin or the printing area that is trimmed off.

The bleed ensures that when images reach the edge of the page, there will be no unprinted edges or white spaces around your page.

2. White space

This is a design principle that means the absence of text or images. Your page layout should be a balance of white space and text or images in the book.

White space is your breath of fresh air, making the page easier to read, drawing the reader's attention to the text or image, and giving a less cluttered feel.

3. Misplaced text

Another thing to watch out for in your book pages is orphans and widows. These are the terms used by typographers to indicate misplaced words above or below a block of text.

A widow is a single line of text that moves at the top of the next page or the next text column. An orphan is a single line of text isolated at the bottom of the page or a paragraph.

These elements decrease the readability of your book because they make the reader pause in the middle of a paragraph, interrupting the flow.

Avoid leaving single lines at the bottom ("orphans") or the top of a page ("widows").

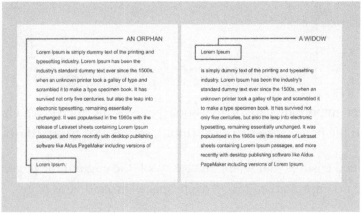

4. Spacing

Line spacing, also called leading, is the vertical distance between lines of text. It helps in the book's readability because it balances the white space between each line of text.

Another aspect of line spacing is the line width, or the width of a block of text or a paragraph, which determines the rhythm and readability of the text.

Some books have text blocks in columns of two, three, or more. Text blocks are harder to read when they are too long, so keeping a shorter line width helps readers keep track of the next line to read.

A dropped capital, also known as a drop cap, is a large capital letter at the beginning of a text block. It usually has a depth of two or more lines compared to normal text and is basically used for decoration and navigation.

A drop cap tells readers that it is the start of a new chapter of the book, which means something new is coming up.

5. Typography

Typography is more than just choosing nice-looking fonts. It's the art of arranging letters and text to make the book more appealing to the reader.

Typography tells a story using font styles, appearance, and text structure. Make sure that your book looks professional and easy to read. Also, the topography should represent the tone of the book. For example, a light-hearted book about dogs may be better represented by a light, airy font type with a lot of white space. Conversely, a more serious topic may warrant a more traditional font and structure.

6. Images

Aside from the text, images play an important role in conveying a message to your readers.

They should come in harmony with typography, text placements, or other elements, especially with the white spaces in your book's pages.

Evenly distribute the images in your book and do not crowd them all together in one place.

Paperback formatting can be a bit complicated, but to make things easy, Amazon KDP has provided an amazing step-by-step tutorial on how to do it.

First, download the paperback manuscript Template here: kdp.amazon.com/en_US/help/topic/G201834230

Next, watch this step-by-step video guide, called "Build Your Book," about formatting a paperback manuscript:

Build Your Book - Format a Paperback Manuscript (Word for Windows) kdp.amazon.com/en_US/help/topic/G202145400

Build Your Book - Format a Paperback Manuscript (Word for Mac) kdp.amazon.com/en_US/help/topic/GLRF8JDXY5LPE3TX

Build Your Book - Format a Paperback Manuscript (Pages for Mac) kdp.amazon.com/en_US/help/topic/G3TQWMMGK8528NDZ

If this is all overwhelming to you, you can find a good layout artist and let them do the formatting for you. You can select from an excellent talent pool in marketplaces using the list on our resource page: Authorsonmission.com/resources.

Again, I highly recommend hiring a professional to ensure a quality product that will attract readers and position you and your brand in the best light possible. Several book formatters on my team have done it thousands of times; just reach out at Authorsonmission.com and inquire about getting in touch with someone.

But as I mentioned earlier, if you choose to do it yourself, there is a simple way using Atticus.

Pro Tip: Formatting is another way to infuse a little bit of your personal style and taste into your book. You can also design your own preferences that will serve as your signature style, yet another differentiator between you and the competition.

Design: How to design your Author website to establish your authority

"Your brand is so much more than what you sell."

—Jon Iwata

Many potential readers want to know your qualities and experiences that give you the expertise to write a book. As we discussed in Step 4 (Positioning), readers want to know the story behind the pen and paper.

Potential readers want to know:

1. Your work or personal experiences that you'll impart in your book.
2. Your credentials and accomplishments that prove you are accurate and credible.
3. Your personality or hobbies that inspired you to write.
4. Interesting facts about you that humanize you to your readers. Relate to them on a personal level.

All of this information should be on your Author Page on Amazon and as part of your author website to extend its reach beyond book sales. Some of those rewards include:

1. Building your authority not only to readers but also to critics, influencers, and media
2. Getting noticed through search engines.
3. Making it easy for people to contact you for interviews or book inquiries.
4. Building your email list for promotions
5. Selling your upcoming books and other products or services

Let's look at the five steps to designing your author website:

1. ***Decide on a Domain Name***

Choose between booktitle.com *or* authorname.com.

Personalize your domain name if you plan to establish yourself as an author and write many books on different subjects. You can also use the title of your book as the domain name.

Just make sure it's short, readable, and memorable.

Purchase your domain name from GoDaddy.com as soon as possible, even if you aren't ready to put content on it just yet. This stops someone else from purchasing it.

2. *Select a Host Provider and Website Builder*

After trying almost all the top hosting providers in the market for my own websites, the one I recommend the most is SiteGround.

SiteGround is noticeably faster and extremely reliable. Their hosting plans are flexible, and their customer support is one of the best in the industry.

Once you integrate your domain name and host, you must install WordPress on your website. The SiteGround support team can install it for you for free.

Once you have WordPress installed, select a website builder to design the pages of your website.

There are several different website builder tools out there. But I personally recommend Brizy, an easy-to-use page builder that allows you to create your author website with its drag-and-drop feature easily.

If you don't know much about coding and designing, Brizy is the tool for you. No designer or developer skills are required.

3. *Build your site's content.*

Creating a simple website can start with just the following pages:

- Homepage with book cover, description, book trailer, reviews or blurbs, and "buy now" button. You can use your book's Amazon affiliate link when linking from your website. An affiliate link is a unique link designated to your book that when a customer clicks through it to purchase your book, you will earn a small commission—every dollar adds up!
- Author Page with bio (250 words) and your photo
- Contact Page with Google map location, email, and social handles.

4. *Set up Your Book's Landing Page*

Your book's Landing Page is where you collect people's email addresses. It should include a hero or attention-grabbing image placed directly below the website header, which will serve as the visitor's first glimpse of you and your book.

To entice them to click, add a "gift"—or, in marketing terms, a "lead magnet." This can be an action guide, a cheat sheet, a checklist, or some version of content related to your book. Make sure it's something that readers will find useful and handy.

For reference, below is an example by James Clear, author of *Atomic Habits*, an author website that is very well done.

5. *Set up Your Email Campaign*

An email campaign is the best way to remain in continuous contact with readers, followers, and, more importantly, potential readers. The goal is to entice people to join your email list and then regularly communicate with them with relevant information and content.

They will begin to look forward to your next communication and what you will be producing next.

Here's an example of an email sequence to help build your list:

- Web visitors enter their email and information.
- They download your lead magnet.
- Email No. 1 – A Thank You message for signing up.
- Email No. 2 – Follow up with another "gift."

- Email No. 3 – Pitch your book by writing "What's in it for you," including a link to a book trailer and the Amazon affiliate link.

Pro Tip: If you do not have the time or skill set to create and manage your author website, be sure to hire a professional skilled in website design to assist you. Your website is a reflection of you, so you want to ensure it accurately represents your personality, expertise, and credibility and encourages readers to stay connected and engaged.

I have listed places on the resource page where you can find the best designers for your author website: Authorsonmission.com/resources.

Key Takeaways: Step 5 - Design

Although the design stage might seem to be the trickiest part of creating your bestseller, when done right, you will reap the benefits of transforming your words into a profitable and highly-rated product that sells!

And isn't that the whole point?

While there were just 4 elements of this step, each one is critical to the success of your eBook and paperback.

Let's review at a high level some of the things we talked about:

- How to Design your Kindle book cover to sell
- How to make a Paperback Cover that will stand the test of time.
- How to format your ebook to keep your readers engaged
- How to design a captivating Paperback layout
- How to design your author website to establish your authority

And, of course, there is always the option of outsourcing to a trusted professional to help you with any or all of these steps to position your book in the best possible light. Please be sure to review some of the resources I mentioned throughout to help you find professionals that best suit your needs for whatever stage you are in.

Don't forget that I am here for you every step of the way and can easily be reached at vikrant@authorsonmission.com.

STEP 6 – DISTRIBUTION

Getting your book out there

"A business is a value creation and distribution process. Before you can sell value to your customers, you have to first create it." — Pooja Agnihotri

As the quote above indicates, before you can sell anything, you must first create it. Well, we have done that and now have a thing of value in your possession. Now, let's move on to all the essentials of distribution or making it available to your customers.

Producing written work is one thing, and you have already proven that you can do that. Getting your book out there is an entirely different challenge, but I will support you in the next few chapters with the distribution of your book.

In this step, I will lay out the essential activities to kick off the actual business of publishing your book.

- How to navigate Amazon's Kindle Direct Publishing (KDP)
- How to find the most profitable Amazon categories
- How to maximize your book's visibility with keywords
- How to publish your Kindle and paperback books with an easy step-by-step guide

- How to publish an audiobook in 3 easy steps

Ultimately, the goal of Step 6 is to get your book in the Amazon marketplace, where readers can easily find and buy it. Although it may seem overwhelming, I will walk with you every step of the way.

Distribution: How to navigate Amazon's Kindle Direct Publishing (KDP)

Kindle Direct Publishing (KDP), initially launched as Amazon's Digital Text Platform in 2007, has become the go-to for potential bestsellers.

Why?

It has the largest reach, easiest access, and widest array of exclusively published titles anywhere online.

With more than 32 million published titles as of January 2023, naturally, you would *want* to be part of this club. Although it might have seemed before you started reading this book that becoming a published author was only a pipe dream, the reality is that getting your book there has never been easier.

The benefits of publishing your eBook and paperback with Amazon DP are boundless.

For your paperbacks:

- With Amazon KDP's non-exclusive agreement, you maintain creative control and own your copyright.
- Your book is set to print on demand. It means that your book only gets printed when someone orders it, so you don't have to keep an inventory of your stock.
- Amazon websites in the US, Europe, and Japan will distribute your book.
- You can earn up to 60% royalties, based on your list price, minus the printing costs.

Pro Tip: You also get to have the option of purchasing your books at a discounted "author price" plus shipping so that you can distribute and sell through other channels, such as sales funnels, book signings, and events.

For your eBooks:

- You get to keep control of your rights, and you can set your own list price. You can even update your book after it's published.
- It will be available on the Kindle Store worldwide right away.
- You can earn up to 70% royalty on sales from your customers in various countries, like the US, Canada, UK, and more. Earn even more through Kindle Unlimited and the Kindle Owners' Lending Library.
- Kindle and the Kindle Store have a broad set of features to use when enrolling your book in KDP, including "Look Inside the Book."

To enjoy these benefits, you'll need an Amazon KDP account.

If you already have one that you use for shopping, it's perfectly fine to use that one.

You don't have to make one exclusively for your book.
Once you're in, you'll enter your author/publisher information in the "(Your Name's) Account" link at the top of the page.

Pro Tip: DO NOT USE a pen name for this for tax and royalty payout purposes.

Next, you'll be directed to the Author/Publisher's Information, where you'll be required to fill out the necessary fields.

From there, you'll be asked to enter payment, banking, and tax info in the "Getting Paid" and "Tax Information" tabs.

When you're done, save and continue.

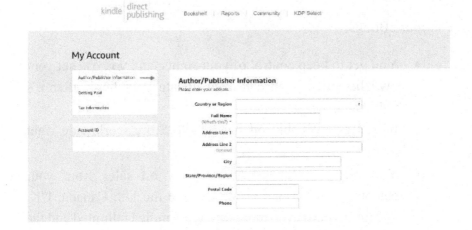

Distribution: How to find the most profitable Amazon categories

The concept of Amazon categories is to organize products to make it easier for customers to find books and products they are interested in.

The idea is similar to a physical bookstore where shelves of books are organized into categories or genres, like self-help, historical, memoir, etc. Only it's a lot more massive.

In the Amazon eBook market alone, 100+ nonfiction categories are further broken down into 1,000+ sub-categories. It is enough to make your head spin.

When you publish your book in KDP, you will be asked to choose three out of 1,000+ categories.

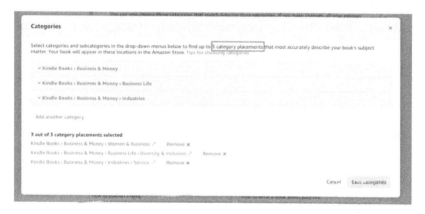

Ideally, you should have a string of categories with keywords that look like this:

Kindle Books > Business & Money > Business Life > Diversity & Inclusion

The strategy is to create a niche for your book through a smart selection of categories to increase the likelihood of your book ranking high on the list.

This hack *makes it easy to become a bestseller.*

Inside this digital bookstore, behemoth are many *categories with little to no competition.* The trick is to find them and be a big fish in a small pond.

You should, of course, make the most relevant category selections for your book so you won't end up disappointing readers.

I highly recommend Publisher Rocket, which you can use to find profitable categories for your book from the 16,000 book and eBook categories.

You can use filters to tell Publisher Rocket if you want to see eBook or book categories, as well as fiction or nonfiction categories. You will also see helpful information, like how many books you'd need to sell to be #1 and #25 in a specified category.

This can help you find the best categories for your book in no time. Follow these steps to find a profitable category for your book or eBook:

1. In the Category Search, select either book or eBook categories.

2. Select a Main Category to look at by clicking **Check it out**.

3. On the **Sales to #1** column, click on the black button to sort the categories from easiest to hardest to achieve the #1 bestseller status. This will show you the number of books you need to sell to get the top spot.

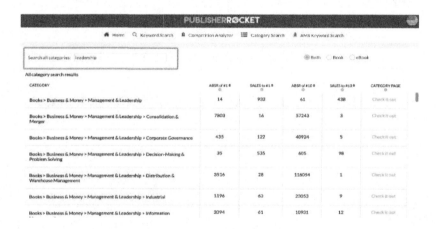

4. To find specific categories that pertain most to your book, type in a keyword on the **Search Categories**.

Your goal should be to find less competitive categories so that it's easier for you to rank #1 in those categories.

Once you rank #1 in a category, your book is automatically tagged by Amazon as a bestseller. And BOOM! You have made it to Bestselling Author status.

Pro Tip: Don't underestimate the power of categories to get you to that bestseller ranking, but do not be fooled into believing that this is the only way or that you should stop reading now. Remember that this is a process, and you must put in maximum effort to achieve maximum results. So, keep reading!

ACTION ITEMS:

Write 3 categories you have selected:

1.

2.

3.

Distribution: How to maximize your book's visibility with keywords

When you go to Amazon to shop for books but don't know the title, what's the first thing you usually do?

Generally, you would go to the search bar and type something that describes your ideal book.

When you hit search, Amazon gives you a list of suggested books related to the words or phrases that you used. Those words or phrases are called "keywords."

Keywords are very important to Amazon and to authors, too.

Like in Search Engine Optimization (SEO), people will type in a set of words to search for options. Amazon uses those keywords to better decide which books it will show customers.

Like any other search engine, you want your book to rank above the tens of thousands of books on Amazon. Being in the top ten of the search results gives your book a bigger chance to get noticed.

As I mentioned when we were discussing the topic or niche to write about, keywords are essential to your overall book publishing strategy. In the Amazon author world, these keywords are known as Kindle keywords and are the words a potential buyer uses to look for a book or an eBook.

Amazon Kindle Direct Publishing (KDP) allows you to choose 7 keywords when you upload your book.

Choosing the most profitable keywords will make your book rank higher than your competitor's book, maximizing its visibility and resulting in more sales.

First-time authors often make the mistake of randomly selecting their seven keywords and categories, and then they scratch their heads when their books don't sell.

I highly recommend Publisher Rocket for keyword research because it provides valuable market data to help you identify the seven most relevant and profitable keywords required to publish your book, including the following.

1. The number of times a certain keyword is typed into Amazon.
2. How much money ranking books that use that keyword are making.
3. How many books are competing for that keyword.
4. Which categories will help you sell more books?
5. How many sales do you need to make to be the new #1 bestseller

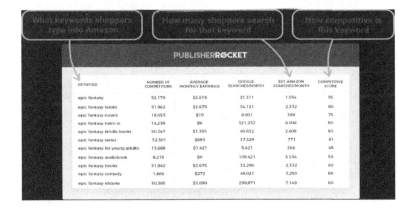

Publisher Rocket is a paid keyword research tool that offers a 30-day Money-Back Guarantee, a fair deal for first-time book publishers.

Start finding your book's profitable keywords by following these 4 simple steps:

1. On Publisher Rocket, click on **Keyword Search**.

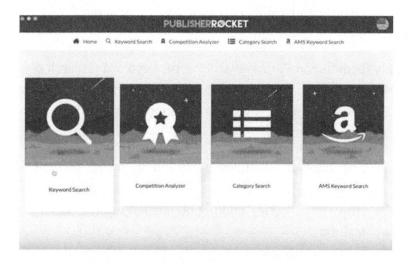

2. Type in a potential keyword for your book. Then select whether this is for your **Book** or **E-Book**. Then click, **Go Get Em Rocket**!

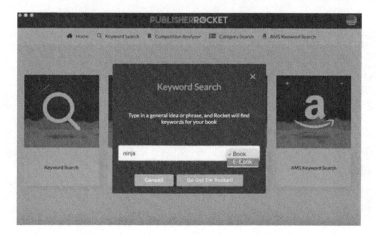

3. Publisher Rocket will then show you other long-tail keywords available. If you are unfamiliar with this term, it simply means a string of words or phrases that are more specific to your book or subject, usually having a higher conversion rate since they are more detailed and specific. Go through the list and select those keywords that describe or relate to your book/ebook by clicking the **Analyze** button.

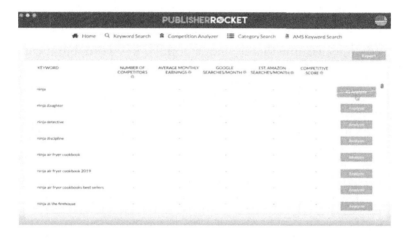

4. It's time to analyze the results. Let's go through each column one by one.

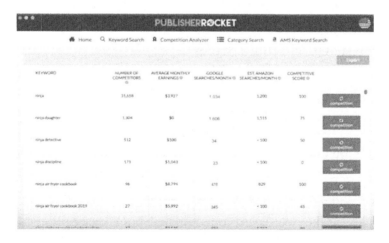

- The **Number of Competitors** shows the number of books that

- pertain to that keyword.
- The **Average Monthly Earnings** shows how much the top 5 books earn for ranking in that keyword.
- For the **Google Searches/Month** and **Est. Amazon Searches/Month**: these columns show the monthly volume for Google and Amazon, respectively. These columns show how popular a keyword is on that platform.
- There are some cases where using the same keyword, people's search in Google yields something, but not in Amazon.
- You may assume that it's not a popular keyword, but it can also imply that these are new book ideas that people are looking for but no one has written about yet.

Pro Tip: This may be your next book's perfect title or subject!

- The **Competitive Score** tells how hard it would be to rank for a specific keyword. The lower the score, the easier it is to rank for that keyword.

Overall, what you would want to know is:

- How much people are willing to pay for the books in a specific keyword (Average Monthly Earnings)
- Which keyword has less competition so you can easily hit the top spot (Competitive Score)

Once you have selected your seven keywords with the help of Publisher Rocket, use these keywords to get your book to sell and rank using the following tactics:

1. Ensure that the keywords are actually relevant to your book.
2. Use the keywords in the actual book title and subtitle.
3. Design a book cover with the updated title and subtitle.
4. Use the keywords in your updated book description to rank higher.

Pro Tip: Remember earlier when we talked about "working title"? This may be a good time to evaluate whether its title and subtitle are appropriate to propel it to the top of the bestseller's list.

ACTION ITEMS:

Use Publisher Rocket (publisherrocket.com) using the strategies above and narrow your selection to the Top 7 Keywords in the right column.

Keyword 1	
Keyword 2	
Keyword 3	
Keyword 4	
Keyword 5	
Keyword 6	
Keyword 7	

You can download a printable version of this Action Sheet at Authorsonmission.com/resources.

Distribution: How to publish your Kindle and Paperback books with an easy step-by-step guide

Unlike the traditional publishing world, Amazon KDP is a very hands-on process. However, it can be overwhelming. But I assure you that I will break it down for you step by step.

Amazon KDP empowers authors to self-publish their books for free in both Kindle and paperback formats. In turn, they earn 35% to 70% royalties from the sale price, depending on whether they sell their books on KDP or KDP Select.

So, now that you have completed the previous five steps in the How to Write a Bestseller process, are you ready to publish your book in Kindle eBook and paperback format?

Let's get started:

25 Steps to Publishing Your Kindle eBook

It is important to note as we dive in that very often, KDP updates its UI/ UX, but overall, you will get the idea of the process through the screenshots below. This information was up to date at the time of publishing but may change at any time, so be sure to follow the instructions on the Amazon KDP website.

On your KDP Dashboard, click on "+ Kindle eBook" to get started.

After clicking on "+ Kindle eBook," a form will open where you must complete all the information about your book, including uploading the actual content and determining pricing, which will be discussed as one of these steps.

Follow the steps below to publish your eBook on KDP:

1. Select the book's Language.

2. Enter the book's Title and Subtitle.

3. Enter the Series Number. (Skip this if your book is not part of a series.)

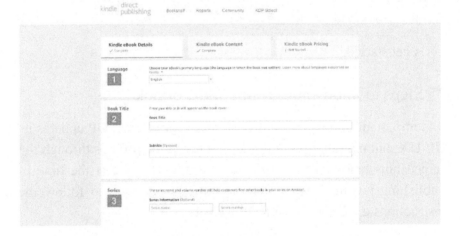

4. Enter the Edition Number. (Skip if your book is the first edition.)

5. Enter the Name of the Primary Author.

6. Enter the Name of the Contributing Author(s), if there are any.

7. Enter the book's Description (4,000 characters max) you created in Step 4 (Positioning).

8. Select "I own the publishing rights."

9. Enter the seven Keyword Results from your Publisher Rocket research.

10. Enter the three Major Categories you have selected through Publisher Rocket as described in the section above.

– See the screenshot of the pop-up window below.

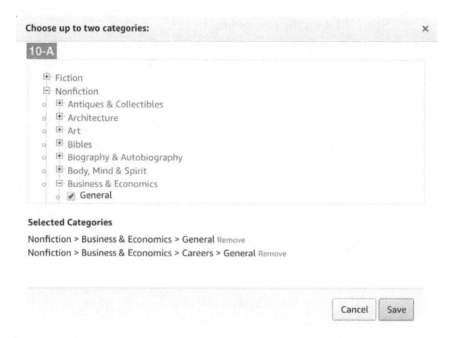

11. Select Age Group. (Skip if not applicable.)

12. Select "Release Now" or "Pre-order. By selecting Pre-Order, you can set the book's release date for up to one year in the future.

13. Save and continue to proceed to Kindle eBook Content.

14. Manuscript:

   a. Select DRM (Digital Rights Management) to inhibit unauthorized distribution and sharing of your book from user to user and device to device.

b. Upload your manuscript. Be sure to follow the steps laid out in Step 5 (Design) for proper formatting of your eBook, but note that KDP also supports any of these file types:
- Microsoft Word (DOC/DOCX)
- Kindle Create (KPF)
- HTML (ZIP, HTM, or HTML)
- MOBI
- ePub
- Rich Text Format (RTF)
- Plain Text (TXT)
- Adobe PDF (PDF)

15. Kindle eBook Cover:

a. Kindle Cover Creator – Select if you want to create cover art in Kindle unless you have already created it in Step 5 (Design).
b. KDP supports any of these file types:
- JPEG (JPEG/JPG)
    - TIFF (TIF/TIFF)

16. Kindle eBook Preview – Click "Launch."

   a. Preview the content on a reading device.
– See the screenshot of the pop-up window below.

17.
    Kindle eBook ISBN

   a. Enter the ISBN. (Skip this part as it's not necessary for eBooks.)

b. Enter Publisher. (Skip this part since you are self-published.)

18. Save and Continue to proceed to Kindle eBook Pricing.

Kindle eBook Pricing

1. KDP Select Enrollment – Opt in to enroll your book in KDP Select to reach more readers.
2. Territories – Select 'All Territories' to make your book available for sale on all Amazon websites worldwide.
3. Royalty and Pricing:

KDP Pricing Support (Beta) – This feature suggests prices for your book based on the sales in the same category as yours.

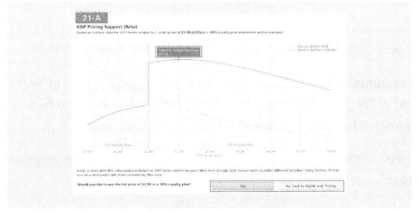

c. Select a royalty plan.

35% Royalty – the Amazon sales commission is 65% for books priced below $2.99 and above $9.99.

70% Royalty – the Amazon sales commission is 30% for books priced between $2.99 and $9.99.

Before we cover the next steps, let's cover some strategies to price your Kindle book.

First, identify why you wrote the book.

- Do you want to earn as much money as possible?
- Do you want to sell as many copies as possible?
- Or do you want to reach as many readers as possible?

Let's break those 3 questions down into 3 price brackets:

If your goal is to maximize the number of units sold	$0.99 - $3.99
If your goal is to have a balance between sales and perceived value	$4.99 - $6.99
If your goal is to build a high perception of your book's value	$7.99 - $9.99

Also, take note that all the prices end in .99.

Studies have found that buyers perceive prices ending at .99 are cheaper compared to those rounded up to the next nearest dollar.

For example, a $5 Kindle book looks more expensive than at $4.99 when, in fact, the difference is only one cent. The .99 price trick is well known to marketers, not just in the publishing world.

Another strategy for first-time authors is to start at a lower price bracket.

If your book starts selling like hotcakes, you can increase its price by a dollar.

If people are still willing to buy and demand doesn't slow down, increase the price even more. When the numbers start to slow down, but people are still willing to buy your book, you've hit the sweet spot.

As you learn and understand the market, you'll discover how your potential readers see the value of your book to better price it and future books. Book pricing has been considered by some an art rather than a science since you must match your customers' perceived value with the value you have put into the book.

As your book's value increases, the book's price also increases.

Now, let's cover the next steps to publishing a Kindle book.

1. Matchbook – Enabling this feature lets buyers of the paperback version get the Kindle version for less or free.
2. Book Lending – Enabling this feature lets buyers share your book with their friends and family.
3. Terms and Conditions – Review the complete KDP Terms and Conditions before you hit 'Publish.'
4. Publish Your Kindle eBook – Congratulations! Your eBook will be LIVE on Amazon in 72 hours.

Pro Tip: As is the nature of technology, change occurs frequently and without warning. Stay current with what the platform offers to take advantage of new opportunities to get your eBook seen, purchased, and recommended.

Although it may seem complicated as you read this, I assure you that if you follow the steps outlined above, you will ultimately be successful at publishing your eBook on Amazon's KDP on the road to becoming a bestseller.

Now, it's time to set up your paperback version.

24 Steps to Publishing Your Paperback

The beauty of self-publishing through Amazon KDP is that publishing a paperback version of your book costs nothing. It only gets printed when somebody buys it, which is called Print-on-demand.

Aside from the many benefits you will reap when you hit bestselling author status, you don't have to worry about moving inventory or any up-front expenses.

After publishing your Kindle book, click on "+ Create paperback."

This will directly link your paperback with your Kindle version and will be much faster since most of the form's content will already be completed.

Follow the steps below to publish your eBook on KDP:

1. Select the Book's Language.
2. Enter the Book's Title and Subtitle.
3. Enter the Series Number. (Skip if your book is not part of a series.)
4. Enter the Edition Number. (Skip if your book is the first edition.)
5. Enter the Name of the Primary Author.

1. Enter the Name of the Contributing Author(s), if there are any.

2. Enter the Book's Description (4,000 characters max) from Step 4 (Positioning).

3. Select "I own the publishing rights."

4. Enter the seven Keyword Results from your Publisher Rocket research.

1. Enter the two Major Categories

2. Adult Content – Yes or No

3. Save and Continue to Paperback Content.

1. Select Free ISBN for Amazon to generate a 10-digit number for your Paperback.

2. Enter Publication Date.

Paperback Content

1. Select Print Options:

    a. Black-and-White Interior

Pro Tip: Select the color option if your images are in color. Note that this will dramatically increase the printing costs since the entire manuscript will no longer be black and white only.

    b. Trim Size as discussed in Step 5 (Design)
    c. Bleed as discussed in Step 5 (Design)
    d. Select Paper Finish – Matte or Glossy
    e. (This is a personal preference for how you want your book to appear visually.)

2. Format Manuscript for Print unless, of course, you have completed the formatting of the manuscript in Step 5 (Design) above:

    a. Upload .doc manuscript file.
    b. Choose a template.
    c. Customize front – title page, copyright, and table of contents pages.
    d. Customize chapter pages – insert your information into the headers and chapter beginnings.
    e. Add page numbers to the table of contents.

f. Review your file.

3. Format Cover for Print. We also covered how to create your own or hire a designer in Step 5. If you have created your cover outside of KDP, be sure to upload it directly into the Cover Creator tool.

    a. Open the Cover Creator tool.
    b. Upload a custom image or select from a template.
    c. Choose a design.
    d. Customize the design.
    e. Preview the cover.

4. Launch Preview for a final look:

    a. Approve the preview of your book to proceed.

Pro Tip: If there are any issues with the format of your manuscript, you will see a message at this point to correct anything BEFORE approving it to move on to publication.

5. Save and Continue.

Paperback Pricing and Royalties

6. Select "All territories" (worldwide rights) if your book is your original content and you've never published it before.

7. Calculate Royalties – Paperback royalty rates are 60% of the list price displayed on Amazon at the time of purchase, minus printing costs, applicable taxes, and withholding.

8. Calculate Printing Cost – KDP prints paperbacks on demand. Printing costs depend on which Amazon website your paperback is ordered from, as well as page count and ink type. Printing cost = Fixed Cost + (Page Count * Per Page Cost).

Be sure to decide on your paperback price before proceeding to the next steps.

Paperback pricing is simpler after you're done with your Kindle Book price. Most authors add $7-$10 to their Kindle Book price to develop their paperback price.

Pro Tip: Check out the price of some competing titles in your genre, niche, and category. This will give you a good indication of the price your target reader is willing to spend on a book of this perceived value and quality.

Based on the Kindle book price bracket, this should be the paperback price bracket.

If your goal is to maximize the number of units sold	$7.99 - $13.99
If your goal is to have a balance between sales and perceived value	$14.99 - $16.99
If your goal is to build a high perception of your book's value	$17.99 - $19.99

If you're wondering about your profit through Kindle Direct Publishing (KDP), the royalty rate is 60%.

Your printing costs come out of that and depend on page count, ink type (black and white vs. color), and the Amazon marketplace your paperback was ordered from.

Generally, if you sell your paperback for $10, your profit will be around $4.

9. Review the Terms and Conditions.

10. Publish your Paperback.

Distribution: How to publish an audiobook in 3 easy steps

Once your manuscript has gone through the approval process and is live on Amazon, you are NOW officially a published author, well on your way to bestselling author status.

To expand your reach, you'll want to consider publishing an audio version of your book as more and more people are consuming audio formats of books on the go.

Smartphones and smart speakers have changed the publishing game, with more audiobooks consumed daily. The audiobook industry is worth 2.4 billion in the US alone, with 80% of the market captured by Amazon Audible.

Since everyone has a unique learning style, audiobooks can expand your reach by 100%, tapping into audiences that eBooks and physical books can't reach.

Here are some benefits unique to audiobooks.

1. Reach a new audience.

Many people want a good story but don't want to or can't read a whole book. People who are too busy to sit down and read can listen to audiobooks on the go.

People with reading disorders and those who have sight impairments can enjoy listening as well.

2. Listen anywhere.

3. Your listeners only need to use a smartphone or laptop they already have with them all the time to enjoy your audiobook. All they have to do is ensure that their devices are powered up and they can listen from wherever they are.Multitasking.

Whether cooking or driving, your listeners can enjoy your audiobook while doing another task. They don't have to worry about turning another page or fixing their eyes on text and images.

4. Complements your Kindle eBook and paperback.

Releasing audiobooks can also increase your Kindle or paperback sales. On average, a Kindle book costs $2.99, a paperback costs $9.99, and an audiobook costs $19.99 to your target audience.

After they have purchased the audiobook, most people see the Kindle or paperback as a big discount and won't mind buying that version, too.

5. Earn more.

According to a study conducted by Pew Research, almost 20% of Americans listen to audiobooks. This number does not even include audiobook listeners from other countries. Imagine how many potential sales you'll gain if your audiobook is available worldwide.

Making an audiobook is optional but can increase your overall earnings and boost your Kindle and paperback sales.

Publishing your Audiobook in 3 Easy Steps

You probably have some questions about publishing an audiobook.

- "Will it cost me an arm and a leg?"
- "How long will it take to produce?"
- "Where do I even start?"

The reality is that creating your audiobook is as easy as creating your eBook and paperback, and there are many flexible options for self-publishing an audiobook.

There are even ways to create an audiobook without doing all the hard work yourself. You can actually produce one with little to no upfront costs.

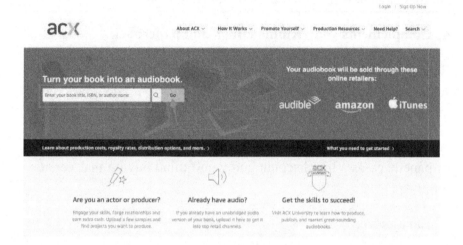

Step 1: Prepare for Audiobook Recording

The first thing you need to do is to convert your manuscript into an audiobook script.

In this step, you'll do away with unnecessary items to generate an easy-to-read version of your audiobook, including:

1. Captions
2. Call-to-action buttons or prompts
3. Visuals
4. Hyperlinks

After removing these items, review the script again and ensure all the content will make sense when converted into an audio format.

Step 2: Audiobook Production

Many options are available nowadays to produce your audiobook, depending on your pace and budget.

When planning your audiobook production, decide who you want to narrate it.

If it's an autobiography, the best person to tell the story is you. You can also opt for a professional audiobook narrator with acting skills.

- ***Record your own voice.***

If you choose to record the audiobook yourself, you can customize it exactly to your liking.

Hearing from the author firsthand is a privilege for most listeners. It's exciting to hear it all from your point of view.

Narrating your own audiobook also takes you and your listeners' relationship to another level.

Consider using a recording studio with all the equipment, software, and a suitable venue for recording. Though it will require some investment, it will ensure that your recording quality is good.

Listeners won't hang in long for a low-quality recording.

When it's time to sell your audiobook, I highly recommend using [Audiobook Creation Exchange (ACX)](#).

To ensure that [ACX](#) will accept your audiobook, you need to meet these requirements:

1. [Audacity](#) – It's a free and open-source digital application software with which you can edit and record your audio.
2. Microphone
3. Pop filter – Also known as a pop shield or a pop screen, this is a noise protection filter for your microphone. It reduces or eliminates popping sounds.
4. Headphones
5. Quiet space

- *Hire a narrator for a fixed rate per audio minute.*

Sometimes, an author may not want to create an audiobook in their own voice. For example:

- o Not fluent speaking in English
- o Does not have the confidence
- o Too busy to do the recording

If you find yourself in any of the above situations or have another reason you don't want to record the audio yourself, there's another way for you to get it done.

You can hire a narrator and pay per audio minute recorded. This means that you will pay the narrator for an agreed fixed rate and won't have to split any royalties with them.

When you hire a narrator, make sure that they can meet the ACX requirements, have the right voice for your book, and can do the audio editing.

The quality of your audiobook will depend heavily on the narrator you choose. That being said, you need to follow a thorough hiring process to find that perfect narrator.

If you are unsure where to find one, I have a list of platforms on our resource page where you can find a narrator for a fixed rate: Authorsonmission.com/resources.

- *Hire a narrator for revenue sharing.*

If hiring a narrator is not in your budget, you can go to ACX and enter a revenue share agreement for no upfront cost.

It will automatically distribute your audiobook through top retail channels like Audible, iTunes, and Amazon.

If you grant Audible exclusive distribution rights, you'll earn royalties of 40%.

Here's how it works: After ACX takes their commission, you and your narrator will split the income in a 50/50 revenue share.

ACX will also handle all royalty payments and any disputes that may arise during the production process.

Because you're in a revenue-sharing agreement, you won't get all the profits. If you spend lots of time and money marketing your audiobook, breaking even might take a while.

Step 3: Upload your audiobook to ACX

The last step of this process is submitting the audio version of your book to ACX.

You might be wondering why Audiobook Creation Exchange (ACX) is on top of my mind when it comes to producing audiobooks.

The reason I highly recommend this platform is that it is the biggest marketplace for all your audiobook needs. ACX is an Amazon-owned website that creates and distributes audiobooks worldwide.

Although you can submit your audiobook to major retail channels like Audible, Amazon, and iTunes, ACX will distribute it for you on those big three.

It works just like Kindle Direct Publishing (KDP) but for audiobooks.

Now, let's discuss how to upload your audiobook on ACX.

Note: You must have a Kindle eBook published to complete this step.

1. Go to the website: acx.com/.
2. Enter your Amazon credentials.
3. Click **Add Your Title.**

4. Look for your eBook on the list. You can also search using your own name.
5. Click **This is My Book.**
6. Click I have this book in audio and I want to sell it.
7. Select your territory and distribution.
8. Choose **World**. Then, choose **Exclusive** for the distribution type. This allows you to get 40% royalties, which is the best deal.
9. Select the language(s) you want to sell your audiobook in.
10. Then click **Continue**.
11. Read and agree to the **Audiobook License and Distribution Agreement** terms.
12. Click **Agree & Continue**.
13. Fill in the **About My Book** section. You can use the content from your Amazon page to do this.
14. Fill in the **Copyright Information**.
15. Fill in the information about your book, the narrator, the audiobook publisher, and reviews and awards.
16. Click **Continue**.
17. Click **Add Cover Artwork** and upload your audiobook cover.

Pro Tip: This may be a great place to outsource the cover design to a professional designer familiar with the specific guidelines to ensure an eye-catching image that meets the ACX requirements. While you can certainly use the cover design from your paperback or eBook, note that the image for an audiobook must be a perfect square, no smaller than 2400 x 2400 pixels.

18. Under the **Upload Your Audio** tab, click **Add Audio File**.
19. Browse for the audio file and upload it.
20. Update the chapter and section titles.
21. Repeat steps 18-20 until all of the files for your audiobook have been added.
22. Lastly, click **I'm Done** in the upper right corner of the screen.

23. Note that the information you have entered for your audiobook, like author name and book cover content, should match what you entered from your eBook.

And you are done!

Pro Tip: Be sure to listen to your new audiobook before uploading it to ACX. Your name and reputation are at stake, and a poor-quality audiobook can be detrimental to your quest to become a bestselling author.

An alternative to ACX for your audiobook is [Findaway Voices](), which, as part of Spotify, has a much broader range of distribution platforms, getting your book heard by many more listeners.

Key Takeaways: Step 6 - Distribution

You have now completed everything you need to ensure your book is available to anyone interested.

You are one step closer to becoming a bestselling author, and now you are ready to reap the benefits of this status, which includes profit, which we will discuss in the next phase.

As a recap, in Step 6, we talked about:

- How to navigate Amazon's Kindle Direct Publishing (KDP)
- How to find the most profitable Amazon categories
- How to maximize your book's visibility with keywords
- How to publish your Kindle and paperback books with an easy step-by-step guide
- How to publish an audiobook in 3 easy steps

So, how does it feel to see the fruit of your efforts on the world's most well-known e-commerce site? I would love to hear your stories of success, the lessons you learned, and any advice you may want to share with others.

I would also love to know your thoughts on how this book helped you get to this point, so please be sure to share them at vikrant@authorsonmission.com.

Are you ready to optimize your book's potential? Let's move on to Phase III.

PHASE III – PROFIT

How to launch the book to bestseller, get sales and reviews, and then monetize from the book

> *"It's rare that I hear the author blame the real culprit: themselves. It's hard to admit but it's the first step toward selling more books and understanding who bears the true responsibility for selling books—the author."*
>
> — *W. Terry Whalin*

We have accomplished so much up until now, and you should be so proud that you have completed the Produce and Publish Phases of the publishing process. Although you have certainly had to put in the effort to this point, here is where the real work will come in to take your book from just being available on Amazon to skyrocketing to that bestselling status.

Let's review the 1-page Bestseller Checklist again to ensure we are on track.

You can download a printable version of the "1-page Bestseller Checklist" at <u>Authorsonmission.com/resources</u>.

We are coming into the home stretch, and in Phase III, we will cover the three final steps to make sure your publishing career gets off to a great start and is followed by sustainable and scalable success in the long term, namely in optimizing your book's potential to earn a profit.

By the end of Phase III, you will learn the following:

- Launch: Essential campaign elements to launch your book successfully
- Marketing: Getting your book into the minds of your potential readers
- Monetization: 7-figure business models to build around your book

So, let's move on to this last phase and optimize your book's potential impact to attract new clients, get paid speaking engagements, and build your brand.

STEP 7 – LAUNCH

Essential campaign elements to launch your book successfully

Book Launch and Book Marketing are both marketing activities intended to increase awareness of your book and persuade people to buy.

The difference is the timing.

Book Launch happens in the first three to four weeks, while Book Marketing is an ongoing campaign to get consistent sales over time.

One opens up the money stream, and the other keeps it flowing.

In this step, you will learn tried-and-tested campaign strategies to launch your book successfully in the market and make it a bestseller on Amazon, including:

- How to create your Author Page
- How to get initial book reviews
- How to make your book a #1 bestseller: A step-by-step blueprint
- How to get more sales and downloads for your book
- How to get 100+ reviews to boost book sales

Launch: How to create your Author Page to Establish Your Authority

The [Amazon Authors Central Page](#) helps authors present themselves to the world and can make a huge difference in the sales of your book.

Why?

Because it lets potential readers know more about you and your legitimacy as an author.

Aside from the logistical benefits of having an [Author Central Page](#) (to track book sales and fix issues with book listings), it's also a great way to connect with your fans.

You'll be able to see and respond to reviews while chatting with your readers. It's like Facebook but for your readers.

Beneath the author's photo is the FOLLOW button. When shoppers click this, Amazon will send them updates about the author, i.e., new releases, reviews, etc.

Your goal in building your [Author Central Page](#) is to get shoppers to follow you so Amazon can do the marketing for you.

Take a look at Simon Sinek's Author Page to help you visualize the content you need to help potential book buyers get to know you:

1. Professional Photo -be sure to follow the same process as described for properly obtaining a headshot for the book cover (Step 4 Positioning)
2. Author's Name
3. Books are available in print, including non-English versions

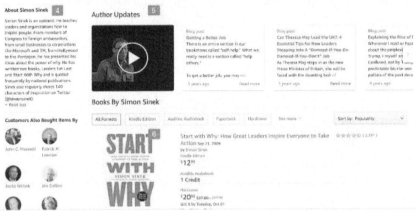

1. Author Bio – a brief, well-written profile with all the relevant info as discussed in Step 4 (Positioning)

2. Author Updates, including links to the author's blogs, social media posts, and book trailers.

3. Add Editorial Reviews – Enter the details, i.e., Reviewer's name, publication, etc.
4. All books by the author are in various formats, including titles in the works.

1.   Amazon Author Rank – the sales of all the author's books on

Amazon.com, which is updated hourly.

You must wait for an email verification when you sign up to create your author page. However, you can start adding info to the page while waiting for it.

Your Amazon Central Page will only become active after you've verified the page via email.

Pro Tip: Follow the same process to set up your international author pages:
- UK - authorcentral.amazon.co.uk
- Germany - authorcentral.amazon.de
- France - authorcentral.amazon.fr

Japan - authorcentral.amazon.co.jp

Launch: How to get initial book reviews

If you get enough people talking about something, the possibilities are endless. In today's digital environment, businesses live or die by reviews posted online.

Like it or not, reviews matter. No matter how single-minded an individual is, most want some sort of public consensus before jumping into a new experience. Think about how often you look up the reviews of a restaurant, vacation spot, or new gadget before buying.

This same concept holds true when choosing a book. Readers are more likely to seek out your book if they have heard or read something about it from someone who has already read it. The more positive reviews you can get, the more readers will be enticed to buy. But getting the right comments and building buzz is not always easy. However, you can take the first steps to establish yourself as a credible author and generate reviews that will highlight you.

Reviews are also an effective way of getting your book ranked—quickly.

The question is, how do you go about getting reviews, especially early ones?

You could do the grunt work of trolling social media sites, author blogs, writer forums, and the like, but that takes so much time and effort without the certainty that it will yield the desired results.

But there is an easier way to get at least 10-15 early book reviews before officially launching your book to the world.

The key is leveraging your immediate circle of influence, like clients, colleagues, competitors, mentors, and people you have helped in the past with your service and advice.

Warning. Amazon's TOS (terms of service) state that no friends and family can review your book. So, it's recommended to avoid friends and family when getting reviews.

Kickstart the process of getting initial reviews for your book by following this step-by-step process:

- Look at the people in your life as potential readers.

- Scroll through the contacts on your phone, email, and social media, and make a list of clients, colleagues, competitors, mentors, and people you have helped in the past with your service and advice.

- Craft an endearing letter or message for each category.

- Instead of providing the direct link to your book, you can ask them to search for the book, typing the keywords on Amazon that will increase your book's ranking for those keywords.

- Aim to get at least 10-15 book reviews on Amazon.

- Make sure to thank your first reviewers for their efforts.

Pro Tip: If no one is reviewing your book, chances are it won't get any visibility in the rankings.

Launch: How to make your book a #1 bestseller - a step-by-step blueprint

The key sales number you need to master to determine your bestseller status is *Amazon Best Sellers Rank* (ABSR). A big number like #100,000 and higher is bad news and means a book is not selling.

You want a low ABSR number to know your book is selling well.

```
Product details
    File Size: 1189 KB
    Print Length: 63 pages
    Simultaneous Device Usage: Unlimited
    Publisher: Dilettante Living Press; 1 edition (October 25, 2015)
    Publication Date: October 25, 2015
    Sold by: Amazon Digital Services LLC
    Language: English
    ASIN: B0176PYTSK
    Text-to-Speech: Enabled
    X-Ray: Enabled
    Word Wise: Enabled
    Lending: Enabled
    Screen Reader: Supported
    Enhanced Typesetting: Enabled
    Amazon Best Sellers Rank: #16,359 Paid in Kindle Store (See Top 100 Paid in Kindle Store)
        #5 in 90-Minute Teen & Young Adult Short Reads
        #2 in 90-Minute Business & Money Short Reads
        #1 in Auctions & Small Business
```

Ideally, your goal is to boost *Sales Velocity,* which means selling more books every day over a period of time (not just during the launch period) to improve your Amazon Best Sellers Rank.

Here are several ways to achieve that goal:

1. Research the Competition

Identify the higher-ranking books in all the categories your book is listed. Then, find out their daily sales average. You can get this data from Publisher Rocket. The screenshot below shows the average number of sales the ranked #1 book makes daily.

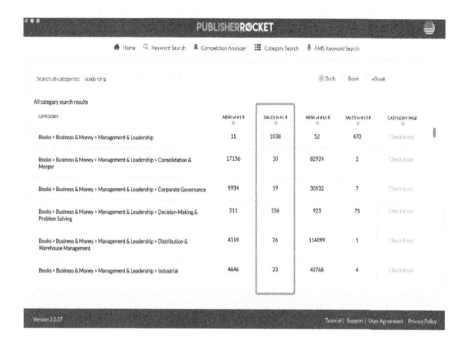

2. Adjust your book's category listing

You can get a sense of the competition by knowing the daily sales average of bestselling titles.

If the sales numbers are out of reach, find less competitive categories to improve your ranking.

Again, you can do this with the help of Publisher Rocket, as discussed in Step 6 (Distribution).

Once you have identified new categories, contact Amazon customer support and request a change in your book's category.
In the screenshot below, you can see that the category "Books > Business & Money > Management & Leadership" has a "Sales to #1" of 1038. This means that the #1 book in this category makes 1038 sales daily. If you're in this competitive category, chances are it will be more difficult for you to reach the #1 ranking.

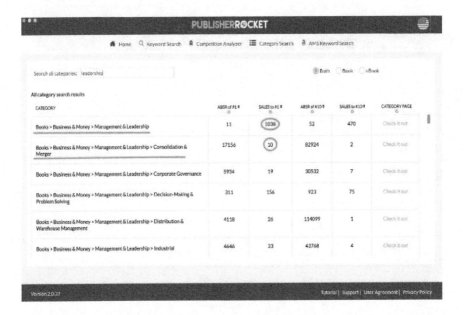

Let's look at another category in the screenshot above, "Books > Business & Money > Management & Leadership > Consolidation & Merger."

It has a "Sales to #1" of 10. This means you'll only need to sell more than 11 books per day to beat the #1 ranking book in that category. This category is less competitive and easier to penetrate than the previous category.

Note that you should only choose categories relevant to your book, not just those least competitive.

Keep scouring Publisher Rocket's search results to find relevant categories that are less competitive.

3. **Pro Tip:** I can't reiterate enough "relevant" categories. Set a Target Date for Getting More Sales Than the #1 Book

Choose a date to run your ads at least three weeks before your book launch to get the maximum sales and surpass the #1 book in your category. We'll talk more about ads a bit later.

For example, if the #1 book gets 200 sales a day, aim to get 201 to become a bestseller.

4. Submit your book to BookBub Marketing

BookBub is a website that recommends books to 3 million email subscribers daily.

There is no guarantee that Bookbub editors will approve your book for promotion on their platform even if you are willing to pay the price (See price guide here), but there is no harm in trying.

Getting your book in front of BookBub readers will definitely accelerate your ABSR.

I recommend reducing the price of the Kindle eBook to $0.99 during the launch period and listing it on other book deal sites, including:

- Freebooksy
- ENT
- RobinReads
- Fussy Librarian
- BKNights
- EReaderIQ
- BookBasset
- BookRaid

5. Deploy Influencer Marketing

Reach out to influencers in your niche for assistance promoting your book. Set a posting date for them to promote your book on their platform—blog, email list, and social.

It is not uncommon for some form of compensation to be asked of you, but it's a small price to pay for the visibility they provide.

There is a platform called Convertkit Sponsorship program, where big influencers, including James Clear, Sahil Bloom, and Pat Flynn, network and help you reach your target audience. I have used this service to promote our clients' books and our service. If you find the right influencer with a similar audience, you can attract many sales during your initial book launch.

Of course, you need to pay fees for the service depending on how extensive the influencer's email list is and how engaged they are, but if you do it right, it will definitely bring positive ROI.

Depending on the influencer, I have paid $1k to $6k per influencer to promote our clients' books. For example, James Clear, who has millions of subscribers, charges a fee of $17k. While this may seem steep, you might consider it if you could reach his audience.

6. Test-run Ad Campaigns

A/B testing, also known as split testing, is used to evaluate the performance of various options. As you did with your title options and possibly keywords, it is important to test out several advertising options to understand which will provide the greatest return and resonate with your target audience.

Set aside a budget, such as $100 per week, earmarked to A/B test several ads on Facebook, Amazon, and BookBub for three weeks to see which ones work.

The next chapter will discuss Amazon and Facebook ads in more detail.

7. Boost Ad Campaign on Launch

Edit your ads according to the results of your tests and reallocate the budget to the more effective ones.

Increase your ad budget one day before the launch to expand visibility and increase sales.

Pro Tip: Amazon rankings can change by the minute, so you'll want to catch your number one spot and disseminate the good news quickly. Be sure to check the ranking in your KDP Author Page often so you can screenshot your bestselling achievement as soon as it happens.

My team at Authorsonmission.com uses the same process to help our Done-For-You clients reach the bestselling rank. If you use this process as outlined in this Launch step, I am sure that you can easily become a bestselling author.

Launch: How To Get 2x More Sales And Downloads For Your Book

Making your way to the rank of #1 bestseller is possible if you follow the steps I have outlined in the 1-page Bestseller Checklist. But, without proper marketing, maintaining the top spot can be challenging.

To stay at the top of the list, it is important to market your book consistently to keep a steady flow of sales and downloads coming and, more importantly, attract new readers.

In Step 8, I will disclose other marketing strategies in detail. In the meantime, I will show you some marketing techniques you can use through KDP Select during your initial book launch.

Exclusive Promo on Amazon [KDP Select](#)

Kindle Direct Publishing Select, or KDP Select, is an optional program that encourages authors to sell exclusively on Amazon by offering special perks and features.

It allows you to reach more readers through Kindle Unlimited (KU), which automatically includes your book upon enrollment.

For a monthly subscription fee, KU subscribers can access more than 4 million select titles in the Kindle Store, including digital books, audiobooks, magazines, and comics. So, it is certainly a place where all the bestselling authors want to be.

An Important Note on Exclusivity:

Enrolling your book in KDP Select means you're making the digital format of your book available **exclusively** on Amazon.

During this period, you cannot sell your digital book outside of Amazon, including your website, blogs, etc. However, you can continue to distribute your book in physical format or any format other than digital.

What's in it for you?

1. Earn higher royalties.

You can earn a share of the KDP Select Global Fund based on how many pages of your book KU customers read. Plus, earn 70% royalty for sales to customers in Japan, India, Brazil, and Mexico.

Learn how to compute royalties for KU.

2. Extend your book's reach to new markets.

Help readers discover your books by making them available through Kindle Unlimited in the US, UK, Germany, Italy, Spain, France, Brazil, Mexico, Canada, India, Japan, and Australia.

3. Maximize Amazon's Promotional Tools.

When your book is enrolled in KDP Select, you can take advantage of Amazon's promotional tools to get more sales and downloads, such as:

4. Free Book Promotion - readers worldwide can get your book free (for a limited time)
5. Kindle Countdown Deals - time-bound promotional discounting for your book while earning royalties

Set up Your FREE BOOK PROMOTION on KDP Select

As part of Amazon KDP Select, you can run a Free Book Promotion, a quick, easy way to boost your book.

You can offer your book for free to readers for up to 5 days for every 90-day KDP Select enrollment period.

You may be thinking, "I am trying to earn a profit. Why would I offer it for free?" Well, check out the following benefits that you can get by offering your book for free:

1. It helps your book move up the rankings so it can get noticed by book buyers after the promotion is done.
2. It can be difficult to sell a book if people know nothing about you as an author yet. A free book promotion lets your book speak for you.
3. It increases your visibility to new readers, especially when you add them to your mailing list. This helps other people learn more about you and your book.
4. You can contact the people who downloaded your free book and ask them for reviews.
5. Free book promotions also help your paid rankings. People who download the free book to their Kindle Unlimited plan get immediate credit for any pages they read.
6. Your readers will look forward to the book's sequel and other future books.

Give your book a boost by starting your Free Book Promotion. Just follow these steps:
1. Go to your Bookshelf and click the ellipsis button (…)

2. Click *KDP Select Info.*

3. Under *Run a Price Promotion*, select *Free Book Promotion*. (*Kindle Countdown Deal* will be selected by default.)
4. Click *Create a* new *Free Book Promotion*.

5. Enter the desired start and end date and click "Save." Avoid ending on *the* final day of your KDP Select term.

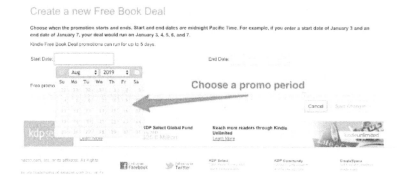

6. Once you have scheduled your free promotion, advertise your offer.

Place your book's Amazon sales page link on as many book promotion sites as possible.

Don't wait until the last minute to advertise. Plan your timeline to let more people discover your free offer.

These book promotion sites have established email lists, social media pages, and groups where they can advertise for you. The goal is to increase the number of book downloads and get some reviews to boost your book's Amazon rankings.

You can find a handy list of reliable book promotion sites (both free and paid) at [The Best Book Promotion Sites in 2023](#).

7. OPTIONAL STEP

Adding your book details on all these sites can be daunting and time-consuming. Luckily, there is a book marketing tool that can help you list your book on promotion sites in just 30 seconds.

Supercharge your KDP book promotions with [KDROI.](#) This browser extension submits your FREE, 99c, or Permafree Kindle book promotion from within your Amazon book page to 32+ book promotion sites.

Set up Your COUNTDOWN DEAL on KDP Select

If you are interested in running a $0.99–$2.99 promotion and your book is on KDP Select, you can also run a Kindle Countdown Deal.

This is different from simply changing the list price for your book. Select "Kindle Countdown Deal" from the dropdown and choose your dates using the same steps as above.

What are the benefits of a Countdown Deal?

1. Even if you are selling your book at a discount for less than $2.99, you still earn a 70% royalty rate.
2. Amazon will promote your book on Kindle Countdown Deals and Kindle Daily Deals pages.

Pro Tip: Create a schedule at least six weeks before your intended book launch to get these marketing techniques in place to build momentum and attract potential readers.

For example, you may want to consider:
- Week 1 to 2 – Run a Free Book Promotion
- Week 3 to 6 – Run a Countdown Deal Promotion

It is also a good idea to submit a promo application to BOOKBUB.

Launch: How To Get 100+ Reviews To Boost Book Sales

We talked about how to get your first 10-15 reviews from your immediate circle of influence, like clients, colleagues, competitors, and mentors, in the "Importance of Getting Reviews" section. Now, we'll discuss how to get more from expert book reviewers.

Reviews are the virtual version of the power of word-of-mouth and play an important role in your book's promotion. More reviews are always better, after all.

As you continue to promote your book, book reviews act as your social proof, also known as trust indicators, and affect a person's buying decision.

As social proof, book reviews help potential readers determine if your book is useful and worth their time.

A good book review should reflect the reviewer's personal reaction, emotion, and experience about the book. If you want better social proof, gather more book reviews.

Aim for quality book reviews written by experienced reviewers.

Aside from being social proof, book reviews also have an impact on Amazon's algorithm, helping your book rank higher than your competitors' books.

As I mentioned earlier, the success rate of your book and, by default, getting reviews will depend heavily on your book cover and description. If neither is appealing, you will not attract reviewers and potential readers. So, be sure you have followed all of the guidance in Step 5 (Design) to ensure these are both on point.

Pro Tip: It cannot hurt to do one final A/B test of several cover designs and book descriptions just to be sure you are on the right track before you put in the effort of launching your book.

Successfully getting influencers and professional reviewers to write a review will also depend on whether you already have some reviews. If you don't have any at all, some reviewers may not be interested—another reason it is so important to get those initial reviews.

Here are two more ways to get reviews very, very fast.

1. Ask for Reviews In Your Book
The easiest way to get book reviews is to ask for them. What better place to do that than in the book itself?

Usually, it's best to include a short, direct review request toward the back of the book since good reviewers tend to read all the way to the end.

2. Try Pubby, Booksprout and BookSirens, which can help you get tons of reviews quickly.

Unsurprisingly, cold emailing to potential reviewers will probably only yield a 10% return. So, let me share some other strategies to help you get those much-needed reviews. These methods will require more time and effort and will be more efficient if you can use the services of a virtual assistant.

One strategy is to get reviews from cousin reviewers, AKA your competitor's book reviewers. These are the people who have already written reviews on books similar to yours.

Start by looking for similar books. Identify the best reviewers and ask them to write a review for you.

Since the weight of this strategy rests on the responses of the cousin reviewers, following up is important.

The first step in getting these reviews is to look for cousin books. These books are within your category, which means you can use your book's keywords to look for them. You can find them using:

1. Search engines

Add the words Best, Top, and Must-haves to your book category while searching for similar books.

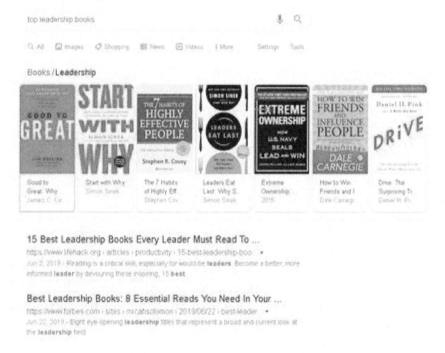

2. Online booksellers like Amazon and Goodreads

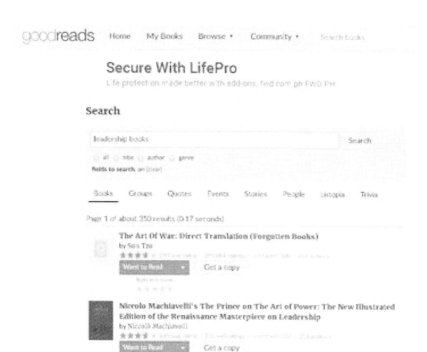

On Amazon, you can refine your search by clicking on subcategories on the left side of the screen.

3. YouTube book reviews

Based on your search results, select books that have high ratings.

Next, look for quality reviews. At first glance, you'll notice a well-written review by its length. Take note of the people who have posted these reviews.

In a spreadsheet, list the names and contact details of these reviewers.

When you look for contact details, don't be surprised that not everyone shares their contact info. Only a few willing book reviewers on Amazon give their website and contact details on their profiles.

If you find their website on their profile, you can use tools like Hunter to get their verified email address.

For YouTubers, check their video descriptions and their About page.

Aside from Amazon and YouTube, you can look for reviewers on social media profiles like Facebook and LinkedIn.

Once you have a reviewer's contact information, you can send them an email or message with the following details:

1. The book title and author's name
2. A short book description
3. Your book's achievements (ranking, number of 5-star reviews, number of copies sold, etc.)
4. The important points of your book in bullet form
5. Permission to send them a free paperback copy
6. Ask for their postal address

Most professional book reviewers have lots of other books to review. It can take a while before your book gets a review.

Follow up every 3-4 weeks, but don't be pushy. If you send a lot of emails for a successive number of days, they might get annoyed and give you a hard "no." Be persistent but patient.

As a way of saying thanks, offer to support their work or give them a recommendation. You can also share their link on your social media platforms to promote their work. Make sure to save your list of reviewers for your next book.

This strategy of searching for reviewers will take time, but it will help you get several reviews, which will eventually get you more sales on your book.

Another strategy to get reviews is to hire someone from Fiverr to reach out to reviewers for you, which will save a ton of time but will add to the expense. As long as you budget for it, I do not see a problem, and the result will certainly help boost your rankings.

Key Takeaways: Step 7 - Launch

While many of the topics discussed in this launch section "look" like marketing strategies, it is important to understand that the two are, in fact, interconnected. Launching your book and moving it to the top of the list quickly requires strategic planning and marketing.

Remember that the goal is to bring awareness to potential readers that your book is out there and persuade them to buy.

In this step, we covered:
- How to create your Author Page
- How to get initial book reviews
- How to make your book a #1 bestseller: A step-by-step blueprint
- How to get more sales and downloads for your book
- How to get 100+ reviews to boost book sales

In the next section, we will dive deeper into steps revolving around marketing and how to help you maintain the success that your launch efforts hopefully bring.

Don't forget that I am here for you and will applaud your efforts every step of the way. Be sure to reach out at

vikrant@authorsonmission.com and share your success so far.

STEP 8 – MARKETING

Getting your book into the minds of your potential readers

The saying goes that having a product without advertising is like winking at someone in the dark. *You* might know what you're doing, but that doesn't mean anyone else does.

Marketing your book is not an easy task. But, in our age of connectivity, it's much easier than before.

Social media is a treasure trove of potential customers eager and willing to share the news of an awesome new discovery. You just have to know how to break through the noise.

Ideally, you want to get your book into the minds of potential readers and get them talking about your work.

I will provide simple marketing tactics to ensure ongoing book sales in this step, including.
- How to get the media buzzing about your book
- How to land Podcast appearances to promote your book to a mass audience
- How to market your book on social media with seven best practices
- How to utilize the power of paid ads

How to leverage influencer platforms for bulk sales

Marketing: How To Get The Media Buzzing About Your Book

The best way to build buzz around your book is through media coverage, just like how TMZ creates buzz about celebrities. But you're not a celebrity, politician, or athlete. So, how on earth can you convince anyone to give you precious airtime?

Hiring a publicist is one surefire way to get attention. It's their job to get the public talking.

Publicists are savvy digital entrepreneurs who know when to strike and speak up. They have the necessary connections to get you out there through various traditional, digital, or social media platforms.

Of course, a major cost comes with hiring a publicist. On average, it costs anywhere between $2,000 and $10,000 per month, but hiring a publicist *will* deliver results.

You can also pitch your book directly to media outlets by writing a press release in the hopes that you get a guest spot on relevant shows, get featured on podcasts and vlogs, or get talked about by influencers.

Reaching out respectfully and concisely gives you the best opportunity to get a response. But remember that these outlets receive hundreds of requests for mentions, so chances are you might not hear back.

However, if your book has great reviews on your Amazon page, there's a bigger chance they'll respond.

Believe it or not, there is a standard to writing a press release. The more you stick to the format, the more professional you look.

And, as a writer, you must be always professional.

Here are a few questions to consider before getting started on your press release:

- Who's going to be the most interested in reading your book?
- Do I have a great hook or headline?
- Does my book answer a current or trending concern or topic?
- Is it powerful enough?

Your press release should include your name, contact info, web or social media sites, a captivating headline, an optional sub-headline, a well-crafted body (content), book cover image and reviews, and an "About the Author" section at the bottom, known as a "Boilerplate."

Use topical and descriptive keywords, correct grammar and punctuation, simple language, and proper voice tense.

The entirety of your press release should address the basic "who, what, where, when, and why" of information dissemination.

Inform people of your book, but don't promote it—hard selling reeks of desperation.

Once you're happy with your press release, get it out there.

Several services can help you disseminate your press release to the necessary outlets. For example, HARO stands for Help A Reporter and Just Reach Out.

You can find journalists who will write about your book and get the word out about you by creating an account and signing in.

I have included an example of a book press release for your reference here.

Marketing: How To Land Podcast Appearances To Promote Your Book To A Mass Audience

I want to share with you another exciting way to promote your book to a mass audience. Although it can be a tedious process to do it yourself, I will pull back the covers and reveal every secret I know to either build the system in-house or hire and train someone to do it for you.

At Authors On Mission, we use a platform called <u>Listen Notes</u>, a subscription-based app, to find relevant podcasts to book our clients. Here are six easy steps to getting exposure to a massive audience quickly and easily:

1. Purchase a premium subscription.

To search for podcasts, as I will describe, you must subscribe to a premium membership, which costs $180/month as of this writing.

2. Search for relevant podcasts

Of course, you can't just speak on any podcast; it must be relevant to your topic or subject. For example, if your book is about leadership, you want to get on active leadership podcasts with a high engagement rate and a listener score of 50 or higher. In fact, the higher, the better because a high score means that listeners are engaged with the content and continue listening longer.

When doing your search through the premium membership portal, be sure to identify those podcasts in the top 5 - 10% range. It will certainly be harder for you to get on any show below 1%, but as you gain traction with the audience, you can target those podcasts in the lower ranges and increase your visibility.

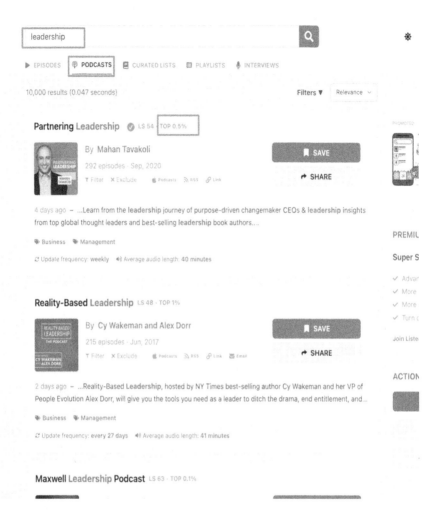

3. Research

Once you identify possible podcasts to reach out to, click on each podcast to learn more about it, understand if your topic is a good fit, and, most importantly, find the email address for the host or manager of the podcast.

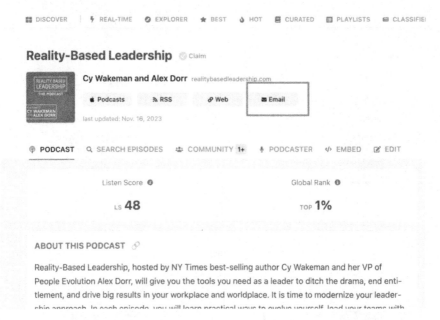

4. Tracking sheet

As you collect data about podcasts and all of the relevant contact information, create a system to track and monitor your outreach and progress. We use a Google sheet that includes the podcast name, the host name, website, social media sites, email link, schedule, topic, etc.

Once the podcast is published, your tracking sheet will be an easy way to manage the links and use them for further promotion.

5. One-page sheet

To increase the possibility of a podcaster inviting you to be on their show, I recommend creating a one-page sheet for quick and easy access to everything they will want to know.

The elements on this sheet should include:
- Your picture
- About the speaker

- About the book
- Suggested interview topics

This sheet will not only give you access to being a guest on a podcast, but hosts will use it once you are booked to introduce you to their audience.

The following is an example of a one-page sheet my team designed for one of our clients:

1. Email pitch

Now is your time to shine and position yourself in a way that entices the host to *want* to have you as a guest on their show. For example, I recommend listening to a few minutes of a recent podcast episode and grabbing some interesting or relevant content that you can use in your introductory email.

I recommend creating two or three email templates:
- Initial email
- Follow-up email to send after two or three days
- Second follow-up email

Here are some things to include in your initial email:
- Introduction, where you indicate the podcast name and that you are a loyal listener
- Some information about a recent episode you have listened to that you gathered during your research
- Create an email/address writing as another person who will be introducing you (the author) along with some quick facts.
- Introduce the idea of having you as a podcast guest.
- Attach your one-page sheet.

It is normal for people not to respond to the first email. Hence, it is appropriate to send a follow-up email several days after the first, checking in to confirm they received your initial email and to schedule a convenient time to be a guest.

Keep your communication as simple as possible and I guarantee it will work; I should know. We have helped our clients get on thousands of podcasts to date.

We have had great success using these email templates and the six steps I have laid out, with approximately 25% of hosts responding and 4 or 5 show bookings, depending on the niche.

Of course, you can certainly do this yourself, but it is also important to note that at Authors On Mission, we can do it for you as well. We focus solely on authors, helping them to maximize their exposure and reach. We do it all for you, including the one-page sheet, the email sequences, and the outreach, getting you on those less than 10% ranked podcasts. If you want us to do it, then you can schedule a call here - authorsonmission.com/call

All you have to do is get on the show and talk about your book and area of expertise. But what is important in doing this is positioning. It can certainly drive a lot of sales and bring many new customers if positioned appropriately.

Usually, podcast hosts ask questions about you, your backstory, and the book, leaving the window open for you to share how listeners can reach you via social media, website, etc. This is also a great opportunity to offer something for free, like maybe a checklist or an eBook when they go to a specific site in exchange for their email address. Again, this is another great way to increase your subscribers and followers, of course, attracting new readers as well.

This has worked very well for us and our clients to get on podcasts and promote their books, brands, and businesses. Remember, if your goal is to get more readers, be sure to talk specifically about certain chapters or subjects to entice a potential reader to purchase it. On the other hand, if your goal, based on your 'why,' is to get more clients, talking about the success stories of clients you have worked with would be more effective.

Marketing: How To Market Your Book On Social Media With Seven Best Practices

Marketing on social media isn't the same for all platforms. Each has a certain approach and tone that is unique.

Applying the best practices of each platform when it comes to book marketing can help you expand your network, bring in more book purchases and speaking engagements, and develop loyal, supportive fans.

Here are seven best practices to employ across social media platforms:

1. Images

When promoting your book, the best images are your image cover, hero image, and pictures from book signing events.

Pro Tip: Be sure to select a hero image that is relevant to you and your target reader.

Each platform has a different image requirement. Make sure to use the right image size on each platform to maximize visibility and shareability.

Watch out also for your color themes. Darker shades work best on all platforms. Save the bright colors for highlighting certain events in your profile.

2. Headlines

Craft an emotional and intriguing headline that will capture your readers' curiosity and make them want to read more about your book.

Customize your headline for your target audience as if you were speaking directly to them.

Be careful when choosing the tone. Think about the trigger words your target readers would respond to.

3. Engagement

Your audience doesn't just want to see your posts. They also want you to interact with them.

When you post, make sure to respond to inquiries or just leave a quick comment. It's a good way to build relationships with your readers and future business partners.

Encourage your audience to tag people and share your book on their page.

4. Timing

Do you get more engagement on your Monday posts than on Fridays?

Keep an eye on your analytics and study the behavior of each platform. This will help you know what days and times to promote your book to maximize reach and engagement.

5. Contests and events

Announcing future events like book signings, speaking engagements, or book launches is a good way to let your readers know what to anticipate.

Pair these events with raffle contests where fans can receive a paperback copy of your book as a prize for simply liking, sharing, and commenting on your posts.

6. Hashtags

Hashtags are words or phrases with a "pound" sign (#) in front of them, used to help people follow trending themes or conversations.

These are very handy across social media platforms when it comes to searchability. And, of course, you want to join in the momentum of any trending topics or discussions.

Choose hashtags that are easy to remember and relate to your book's niche, topic, category, or keyword.

You may think, "How do I know which hashtags to use?" This is where the research you have been doing will be helpful. You have already talked to influencers, done A/B testing, and researched keywords. Why not use some of this intelligence to help guide you in which hashtags are popular or trending?

7. Linking

Across your social media platforms, link each of your accounts. For YouTube, make sure to add the links to your Facebook, Twitter, and Instagram profiles in the description of every video.

This makes it easy for your audience to find you on the social media platform that is convenient for them.

Optimize your profile by adding your credentials, contact details, and other information about yourself. Always keep your profile current and active by sharing the same topic on all platforms.

Below are the top 3 social media platforms to use to establish your connections, build your brand, and promote your book:

Facebook

With 2.3 billion monthly active users, Facebook is the biggest social media platform. It gives you a lot of room for networking and marketing your book.

- Use a Facebook page instead of a personal profile, which is likable, shareable, and easier to promote than a personal account.
- You also get access to your analytics to see which posts had better engagement and reach.

- Maximize your cover photo by adding the image of your book, upcoming events, and contact details.
- You can also include a video intro, a book trailer, a link to your shop, and a "like, share, and comment" contest.
- Ask for reviews. Don't wait for people to write a review for you; reach out to them and ask them to write one.
- If you have the money to spare for marketing, run Facebook ads, which we'll talk about in just a minute, to reach your target audience.

YouTube

With 1.9 billion monthly active users, YouTube is the second-largest social media site.

Owned by Google, YouTube is also the second-largest search engine after Google. You may want to consider this in your Search Engine Optimization since YouTube videos are searchable on Google.

- Create a book trailer for your upcoming book, as mentioned earlier. Share something about the book, like the scene, the main characters, or the music that sets the book's tone. The idea is to tease your readers about the book without spoiling it.
- You can also upload your intro video discussing you as an author. Talk about your writing inspiration, your hobbies, or the kind of music you listen to when writing your book.

LinkedIn

LinkedIn is a great place to establish connections and build your brand. While Facebook has a friendly atmosphere, LinkedIn is more buttoned-up and professional.

To create your online resume, you can add your previous written works, experiences, and skills to your LinkedIn page. Unlike Facebook, Instagram, or Twitter, LinkedIn profiles are searchable on Google.

- Choose a title that best describes who you are and what you do.
- Add your book as a job experience by typing "Author" in the role and the title of your book as your company. Include the dates that you worked on the book. You can also add a short description of the book, the link of the book to your shop, and reviews written by other writers, editors, publishers, and influencers.
- Build your connections and endorse others' skills.
- You can also join author groups on LinkedIn to share your ideas and struggles with fellow authors.

Pro Tip: While these are just some of the social media platforms, it is important to post and engage with your target readers where THEY hang out. If your audience is young readers, in the Young Adult genre, for example, it may not be advantageous to use LinkedIn, which is geared toward an older, more professional audience.

Marketing: How To Run Amazon And Facebook Ads To Get 5x Book Sales

While social media and press releases are some of the free marketing techniques used to enable authentic interactions, paid marketing focuses on customizability.

Paid marketing can help you scale your book sales while giving you full control over targeting your potential readers.

With paid ads, analytics are available to track your reach, engagement, and conversion. You get a bird's eye view of which areas in your marketing approach need improvement and which are working well. It is a similar approach to A/B testing, although you are paying for the information.

I personally prefer paid ads to free marketing because they can increase your sales faster and are more customizable.

In this chapter, we will focus on Amazon and FB ads because they are the main sources of book sales from paid advertisements.

Other paid advertisements like BookBub ads, Google Adwords, or YouTube ads can also increase sales, but Amazon Ads and Facebook ads are the most sophisticated.

How to drive more book sales with Amazon Ads

If you sell your book on Amazon, you might as well advertise your book using Amazon, too.

With more than 300 million users worldwide, Amazon knows a lot about the purchasing habits of its shoppers. After all, its main goal is to match user search inquiries with the products they are most likely to purchase. No wonder Amazon knows so much.

What are Amazon Ads?

Amazon ads work like Google Ads. Type a keyword in the search bar and Amazon searches for products that pertain to the keyword.

The top results are mainly sponsored posts, also known as Amazon ads. You can spot these ads because the word "sponsored" appears just above the product name.

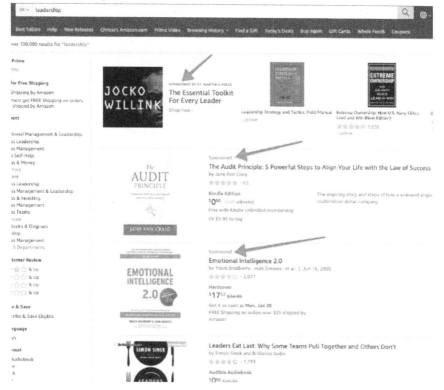

If you want your book to gain more visibility on Amazon, you'll be bidding for a position based on your chosen keywords. Every time a prospect clicks your ad, Amazon will charge you based on your cost-per-click rate, which is calculated as the total ad spend divided by total clicks.

Why Amazon ads?

If your marketing efforts seem to progress slowly and you're not getting quality leads, Amazon Ads take your ad game up a notch.

Running an ad campaign might seem complicated. But don't worry; once you understand what it is and how it works, you'll see why it's all worth it.

Here are the reasons you should advertise with Amazon Ads:

1. Amazon is a worldwide online marketplace. Your book has the opportunity to reach multiple marketplaces 24/7.
2. You can promote your books next to similar books and authors. Letting Amazon do this for you will help you become more visible to potential buyers.
3. Customize your targeting options by book genres, titles, and authors. You can also select different ad types to suit your book advertising strategy.
4. Amazon ads can serve as teasers for your upcoming books. Running ads for your new books helps you drive sales as soon as they are published.
5. You can also run a backlist ad campaign to promote your older titles to a new set of prospective readers.

Amazon Ad Types

1. **Sponsored Products**

These ads appear in the search results and look like a regular product listing. The difference is just the "sponsored" label.

These ads work on a cost-per-click pricing model. Amazon charges you every time a customer clicks your ad. After they click the ad, your customers will be taken to your product's detail page. Amazon uses keyword-based targeting to match users with products. The more popular a keyword, the higher you need to bid to move your product to a better position.

Sponsored products can target your customers based on your selected keywords. You can manually choose keywords or let Amazon do the selection process for you.

Pro Tip: Why not use the keywords you have identified through Publisher Rocket?

These ads work best for customers who are already in the decision-making process. The minimum cost-per-click is $0.2, while the minimum daily budget is $1.

2. Lockscreen Ads

Lockscreen ads also work on a cost-per-click basis. These ads appear on the Kindle e-reader, Fire tablet wake screen, and home pages as full-screen ads when the device is locked.

Full-screen ad on locked Kindle E-readers

Banner ad on the Kindle E-reader homepage

Full-screen ad on Amazon Fire Tablet in full-color display

When the device is unlocked, it appears as a banner ad on the user's home screen. Users who tap your ad on their device are directed to your eBook's detail page.
Remember that Amazon often changes the UI/ UX of its ad platform.

but the basics would be the same. So the screenshots I have shared will help you navigate Amazon ads but may not always appear the same as in this book.

Setting up your Amazon Advertising account

Amazon Advertising, formerly Amazon Marketing Services, offers pay-per-click (PPC) ad options for advertisers, including authors. Follow these steps to start advertising your book:

1. Set up your account on Amazon Advertising. Go through this link and click **Get Started**: advertising.amazon.com/kdp-authors

2. Click **I have a KDP account**.

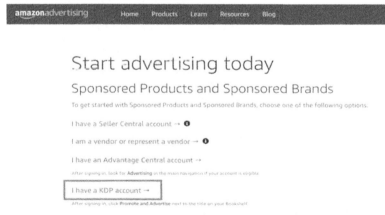

3. Find the book you want to advertise and click **Promote and Advertise**.

4. Choose a marketplace and click **Create an Ad Campaign**.

5. Choose a campaign type. Use Sponsored Products to promote both eBooks and paperbacks. Use Lockscreen Ads for eBooks only.

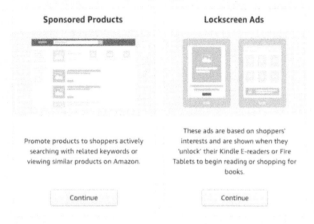

How to create a Sponsored Products campaign

1. Go to **Campaigns**, click **Create campaign**, then click **Sponsored Products**.
2. In the **Settings** section, enter the following information:

Create campaign

Settings

Campaign name
Book 1 Campaign

Portfolio
Books

Start: Jan 14, 2020
End: Jul 31, 2020

Daily budget
$ 20.00

Targeting
● Automatic targeting
Amazon will target keywords and products that are similar to the product in your ad. Learn more

○ Manual targeting
Choose keywords or products to target shopper searches and set custom bids. Learn more

- Campaign name: Choose a campaign name that reminds you of your ad metrics when you started the campaign. The template is [Short Book Title] +[dd.mm.yy]. The campaign name is only visible to your Campaign Manager, not your potential readers. You can't edit it once submitted, so choose a campaign name wisely.
- Portfolio: This tool organizes campaigns to meet your advertising needs. This will help you improve your campaign performance by making workflows manageable. You can create portfolios by brand, product category, or season to help you manage your advertising activities. Organizing campaigns allows you to track performances and view your spending allocation per portfolio.
- Start and End Date: Indicate the duration of your campaign by selecting the start and end dates. You can set your campaign to start immediately or at a future date. Your campaign can also run continuously by not indicating an end date. You can pause your campaign at any time and start it up again later. If

your campaign works well, you can extend its duration by updating the end date.
- Daily budget: This is the amount you are willing to spend on a campaign per day. It is distributed each day in a span of one month.
- Targeting: With this tool, your ads will show up to your target readers using the keywords selected in your campaign. You can choose the keywords manually, or you can let Amazon choose the keywords for you.
3. Choose a **Campaign Bidding Strategy.**

If you are new to Amazon ads, you can leave it at default—Dynamic bids. With Dynamic bids, Amazon will adjust your bid according to the chances of getting a sale.

Campaign bidding strategy

◉ Dynamic bids - down only
We'll lower your bids in real time when your ad may be less likely to convert to a sale. Any campaign created before April 22, 2019 used this setting. Learn more

○ Dynamic bids - up and down
We'll raise your bids (by a maximum of 100%) in real time when your ad may be more likely to convert to a sale, and lower your bids when less likely to convert to a sale. Learn more

○ Fixed bids
We'll use your exact bid and any manual adjustments you set, and won't change your bids based on likelihood of a sale. Learn more

⌄ Adjust bids by placement (replaces Bid+)

4. Select an **Ad format.**

Ad Format

○ Custom text ad
Add custom text to your ad to give customers a glimpse of the book. Limit one product per campaign.

◉ Standard ad
Choose this option to advertise your products without custom text.

- Custom text ad: Using this ad format, you have to include an ad copy to make prospective readers click and direct them to the details page. Make sure to match your ad copy with the language of the Amazon site where you place it.
- Standard ad: You can launch a campaign quickly without a customized ad copy.

5. Create an **ad group**: Add a title for your ad group. This feature is only available in the standard format.

6. Choose the books you want to advertise.

7. Enter your chosen keywords and your bids.

8. Review your ad before you submit it. If you think something is missing in your ad, you can either cancel everything or save all the information as a draft and return to it later. When you're ready, click **Launch campaign**.

How to create a Lockscreen Ads campaign

1. Go to **Campaigns**, click **Create campaign**, then click **Lockscreen Ads**.

2. In the **Settings** section, enter the following information:

- Campaign name
- Start and End Date
- Lifetime budget: This is the maximum amount you are willing to spend for the entire ad campaign. The minimum total budget is $100, but Amazon only charges you for the clicks you get on your ad.

- If your goal is to produce clicks as fast as possible, and running out of budget before the end date is not a problem, select *Run campaign as quickly as possible*. If the goal of your campaign is throughout the entire campaign dates, select *Spread campaign evenly over its duration*. Remember, you cannot change this setting after you have started your campaign.

![Create campaign settings screenshot]

3. Pick out the books you will advertise.

4. Choose the related interests/genres you want to target. You can target as many interests as you want on a single campaign.

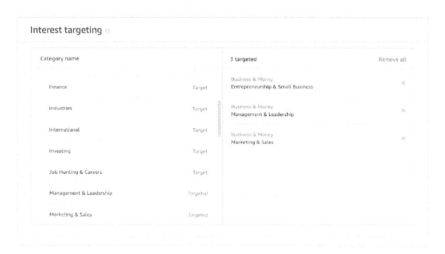

5. Indicate your bids.

Enter custom text that will help you attract readers. The text has to be at least 50 characters and should not exceed 150 characters. Avoid unsubstantiated claims and do not use all caps.

255

6. Review your ad before you submit it. If you think something is missing in your ad, you can either cancel everything or save all the information as a draft and return later. When you're ready, click on Submit for Review.

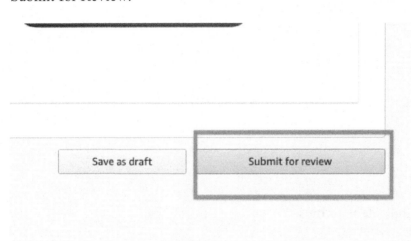

Pro Tip: Remember, if your ad is approved, you cannot edit certain details, like your landing page, books, or ad creative. If you need to make changes, archive that campaign and create a new one.

Amazon Ads can help drive more sales to your book since, being a worldwide online bookseller, it can bring you closer to your potential readers.

You can choose from different ad types to promote your book and target them using specific criteria. Your campaign results will depend on your targeting strategies, so testing your ads is vital to your campaign success.

I recommend conducting A/B testing on your ads to see which ones perform best. Increase the budget of the ads that show a positive return on investment and end the ones that are not performing well.

The marketing team at Authors On Mission also offers Amazon Ads services, so in case you don't want to learn Amazon ads yourself, you can also call us and see if we are a fit to work with you on the Amazon Ads for your book.

Leveraging Facebook Ads (now Meta Ads) to widen your book's reach.

Facebook is an effective book advertising platform because it is so popular with readers.

With Facebook's targeting options, you can promote books specifically to readers who are already interested in a particular author or to entirely new readers.

What are FB Ads?

FB ads are Facebook's way of putting your book right in front of prospective readers. These ads can appear on News Feeds on both desktop and mobile.

FB Ads can laser-target your audience. They have built-in tools to help you create and run your campaigns and generate reports to see which campaigns perform best.

Why FB Advertising?

Facebook has more than 2.3 billion monthly users, almost 1.6 billion users every day, and 70% of that number check their account every single day.

Imagine if you can tap into even a small part of that number. You can build better connections for your books with your potential audience.

1. FB Ads help you drive more traffic to your author website. When you post great content on Facebook, people will likely click on your link to find more information about your book.

With more visitors to your website, you can turn a cold audience into a warmer audience.

2. You can learn more about your audience through Facebook Insights, an analytical tool to see how your audience interacts on your FB page.

3. If you have already conducted a campaign and were unsuccessful, you can use engagement retargeting to re-engage your audience with your book. You can adjust your parameters by Behaviors, Interests, and Job Titles.

4. You can start building your email list by using Conversion Ads. You can use this strategy by presenting a freebie or a giveaway in exchange for an email. You can offer a freechapter, a book discussion guide, a checklist, or something that supplements your book.

5. When it's time for your book launch, you can use the traffic objective to send people to your website or Messenger. With this objective, you can optimize your ad to get the cheapest cost per link click. You'll need to prepare a short copy for your book launch announcement and a 1200 x 628-pixel image for your ad.

6. Just like Amazon Ads, Facebook or Meta ads also often change the UI/ UX of its ad platform. But the basics usually remain the same so the screenshots I will share below will help you navigate Facebook ads but may not always appear the same as on the screen.

Creating a Facebook page

Before you can run your ads, you need to create a [Facebook page](). You can create ads from a personal user interface, but it is less efficient and powerful than a Facebook page.

1. Go to [facebook.com/pages/create]().

2. Click Get Started on the page type you want to create.

3. Fill out the required information.

4. Upload a profile and cover photo for your page.

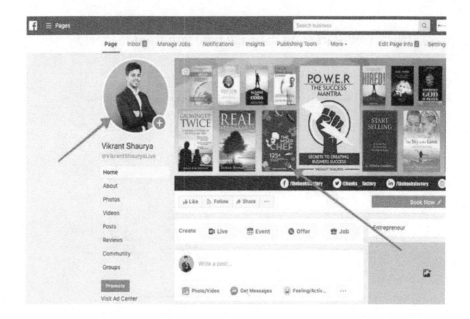

Creating your first Facebook ad

Before creating your first ad, ensure you're using the Google Chrome browser, which accesses the maximum level of functionality for Facebook ads, compared to other browsers that tend to crash while in the middle of creating an ad.

Get Google Chrome for free here: google.com/chrome.

Here are the steps to create an ad:

1. Open the Facebook page where you want to run the ad. Go to Ads Manager and click **Create**.

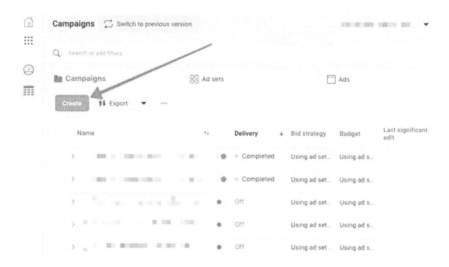

2. Name your campaign and select your campaign objective.

3. Create your audience. Go to the Audience section and select the key demographics (location, age, and gender) of your target audience.

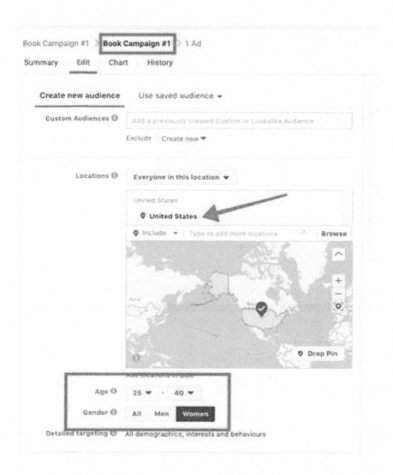

4. You can further refine the group of people to whom you want to show your ads by using **Detailed Targeting**.

Let's take this screenshot as an example. Suppose your book's topic is Transformational Leadership and Strategic Management. You can specify that on the Interests to target that audience.

5. Trim down your audience size. It's easier to work with a narrow audience. The ideal target size is within the green zone. Include all characteristics of your ideal audience to decrease the audience size. You can also do split tests for different interest segments instead of trying to fit them all in the same ad set.

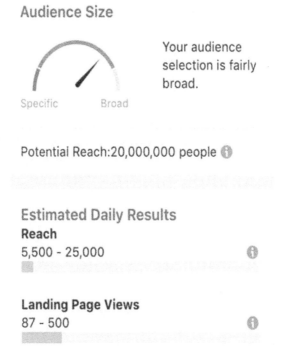

Set the budget and schedule for your ad. Choose between a daily budget or a lifetime budget. A daily budget will run until you have spent the allotted amount each day. A lifetime budget will run for a specific period and stop once fully consumed.

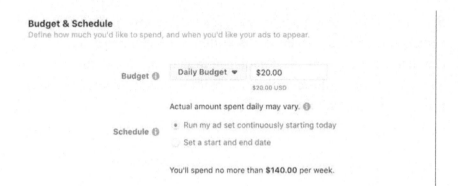

6. Automatic placement is the default setting, but I highly recommend customizing it. Edit the placements by removing Instagram, Audience Network, and Messenger. Focus only on Facebook. You can also do a split test to see which placement works best for your book.

7. Create the actual ad that will appear to your prospective readers.

a. Create a brand-new ad, use an existing ad, or use a mockup.
b. Select an ad format – Single image/video, Carousel, or Collection.
c. Upload your media files for the ad. Make sure the text you place inside the image does not exceed 20% of the image itself.

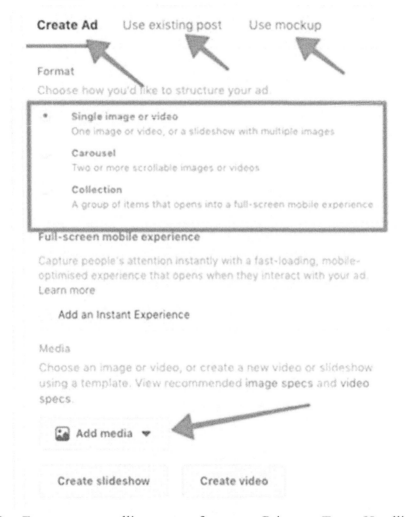

8. Enter a compelling copy for your Primary Text, Headline, Description, and Website URL, and select a Call to Action.

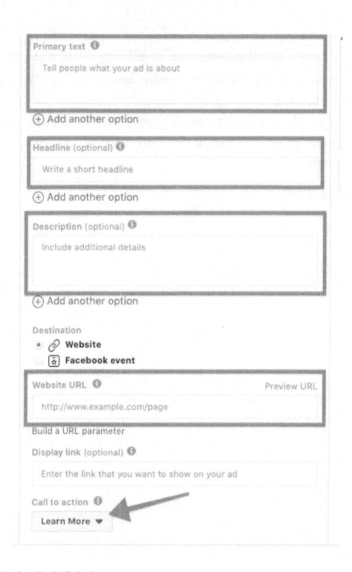

9. Hit the **Publish** button.

_____*Note:* Facebook frequently changes its UI/UX for its Ad Manager. If you find the guidance in this book slightly different from the Ad Manager interface, don't worry. Just keep the basic ideas of this guide in mind.

Four Ad Types that are best for your book

If you are still wondering what strategy to use for your book, I've narrowed it down to four ad types, which will accommodate different authors with varying goals.

First, you need to determine three things:

- What do you want your readers to do after reading your book?
- When a person clicks your ad, where do you want them to go next?
- Aside from book sales, what other goals do you want to achieve by promoting your book?

Once you have identified these three things, it's time to choose your ad type.

1. **Boosting a post with good content.**

If you have a blog or good content hiding in your website, use Facebook ads to direct people to it so you can start connecting and engaging with them. The idea is to build credibility and trust so potential readers become excited about buying your current and future books.

You can also run a Facebook Live video to discuss parts of your book or supplementary ideas around your book topic.

After posting your content, click on **Boost Post**.

Use Engagement targeting when promoting your book to re-engage with previous connections.

When boosting a post, you can specify keywords to target people in your genre or similar authors.

2. **Build your email list using Conversion Ads.**

Selling a book for $1.99 to a cold audience on Facebook will not be easy. It's like selling ice to an Eskimo. You'll be lucky if you get a positive ROI from a Facebook ad.

The solution to converting a cold audience to a warmer one is to move potential customers down the funnel toward purchasing by adding them to your email list.

Before sending them newsletters and promotional emails, you must know how to build an email list using conversion ads.

On your conversion ad, you'll have a Call to Action that says "Download." Your readers will click here to download your freebie or giveaway in exchange for their email addresses.

Make sure that you have installed Facebook Pixel on your website so your tracking is ready.

Go to your Ads Manager and run a conversion ad on the page of your website where the freebie or giveaway is located.

3. **Advertise your Book Launch using Traffic Ads.**

If you aim to create a big impact on your book launch, use the traffic objective to help you optimize your ad while getting the cheapest cost per link click.

But first, you'll need to create an image that is 1200 x 628 pixels with 20% text.

With the traffic objective, add the targeting for your ideal readers.

Write a compelling copy that tells your audience about your book launch and includes great reviews.

4. **Promote your Book Launch or Book Signing through Events**

Ads.

Let people know you're planning a virtual launch party using event ads designed to help you increase awareness about your upcoming book event.

Take note that you can find the Event Ads within the Engagement objective.

Pro Tip: Testing is key to the success of Facebook Ads. It is important to run several ads, targeting options, images, and ad copy combinations simultaneously to see which performs best. End the ads that are not performing well and run only those that obtain positive ROI.

Marketing: How To Collaborate With Influencers For Bulk Sales

Have you heard of the Oprah effect?

It's a phenomenon that dramatically increases a product or book's sales after a recommendation from a person of high authority or influence.

It's a great opportunity for authors to partner with celebrities and public figures to promote their book.

Of course, you don't really have to reach out to Oprah to get the boost you need. What you need is someone with clout in your target niche and a massive following—an influencer.

What is an influencer?

An influencer is a person whose words carry much weight to those who follow them.

This person has generated many followers who respect what they say. It could be anyone who has the knowledge, authority, social standing, and relationships that impact other people's decisions.

In every niche and industry, there are influencers who have motivated and moved millions of people worldwide. These people typically have their own platforms where they stand out, and their opinions are valued.

You will notice them in:

- Personal pages on [Facebook](), [YouTube](), [Twitter](), [Instagram](), etc., where they have large followings and subscribersOnline communities ([Facebook]() or [LinkedIn Groups]())

- Podcasts
- Local positions
- Popular websites where they get loads of traffic
- Owning successful businesses in certain industries
- Online and offline events

How does your book benefit from leveraging an influencer's platform?

1. When an influencer posts about your book, you get a promotional boost. Depending on how influential the person is, this can directly lead to more book sales.
2. The people who follow the influencer convert from a cold to a warm market easily. The influencer helps build awareness and credibility between you and their followers.
3. Asking an influencer to encourage people to look at your book creates a better relationship between you and the influencer's followers. Knowing that you and your book exist drives more traffic and engagement to your platforms, like your author website, Amazon product page, and social media pages.
4. Give an influencer free copies of your book, and, in exchange, ask them to give you a book review.

Promoting your book can also help the influencers:

1. Influencers look for ways to provide value to their audience.
2. One of the problems you can solve for an influencer is to keep their content fresh and engaging. Position your book as a source of fresh ideas and good content.
3. Another benefit you can give to influencers is to sponsor free books on their platform.

One good example is to give away three free copies of your book during an online event. The influencer picks a winner through a raffle or a contest.

In this way, it'll be a win-win situation for you and the influencer. Your book is promoted, and the influencer offers value to their audience.

The right way to reach out to influencers

If you seek to leverage an influencer for your book promotion, you must know how to find and approach one.

Step 1: Research the influencers and their audience.

Before you reach out to influencers, make sure you do your research. Learn their niche, the kind of people following them, and their goal.

Find out if this is strategically advantageous for your book. You'll get more book sales if your book's topic supplements a group's goal and niche.

For example, if your book's topic is pet care, you'd rather go to influencers whose followers are pet lovers instead of those into make-up and beauty.

There are some platforms like Heepsy through which you can easily find influencers on Instagram, TikTok, and YouTube that will make the entire research process very easy because you can find relevant influencers with the # of followers and engagements. You can see all the data in just one place.

Once you find them, you will want to learn more about the influencer. What topics do they love to discuss? How can you support them? What topics do they need for their next content?

Step 2: Introduce yourself.

Now that you have enough information about your target influencer, create a connection with them by supporting their work on social media, either publicly or in other meaningful ways.

Don't just pop up in front of them and ask them for a recommendation. Instead, give value first and the rest will follow.

Here are some things that can provide value:

- Like, comment, and share the influencer's posts on social media for months or even years.
- Drop a question or takeaway in the comment section of their blog post or YouTube videos.
- Write and publish reviews for their work.
- Offer to write a guest post.

Step 3: Contact the influencer through their preferred channel.

There are ways you can properly contact an influencer. It may be through email, call, or an office visit. Check out their site, social media page, or video descriptions to see which will work best for both of you.

Find out where they are most active and continue to establish that bond.

Step 4: Do a follow-up.

Keep your follow-ups short and simple and avoid being annoying. Start with 1-2 follow-ups.

After 1-2 weeks, send an email to see if the influencer has received the information and offer to answer questions if there are any. Be sure to show your gratitude for any response. And if they say no, don't argue with them to try to get a yes.

When someone shows an interest in your book, shares your content, writes a review for you, or recommends your book, always remember to thank them.

Even if influencers are not that influential on a bigger scale, there could be people surrounding them who have the potential to drive readers to your book. Or, who knows, maybe they could become the next influencer themselves.

The bottom line is always to show appreciation. It always helps and never hurts.

Key Takeaways: Step 8 - Marketing

The term "marketing" can seem scary if you are unfamiliar with how it works. However, I hope the tactics I have defined to get your book into the minds of potential readers have given you the peace of mind to know that you can do it.

The goal is to get people talking about your book and share their reviews, comments, and responses with others. The most efficient way to increase awareness and, therefore, increase potential book sales is to develop a repeatable marketing strategy.

Let's review those actionable steps that have worked for me, helping me to become a bestselling author, and which I know will guide you to achieve the same status:

- How to get the media buzzing about your book
- How to land Podcast appearances to promote your book to a mass audience
- How to market your book on social media with seven best practices
- How to utilize the power of paid ads
- How to leverage influencer platforms for bulk sales

The marketing industry, social media platforms, and Amazon KDP itself are in a constant state of change. I would love to hear about new tools and systems that work for you and help propel your book to the top of the bestseller list. Please send your accomplishments and strategies to me at vikrant@authorsonmission.com.

STEP 9 – MONETIZATION

7-figure business models to build around your book

Never lose sight of why you're putting a book into the world, and you will continue to reap the benefits of its success long after its launch. It is a gift that will keep on giving.

Monetization is a strategy used to generate revenue or additional income from an asset, or in this case, your book. Isn't the ultimate goal of achieving bestselling status to earn a profit? Well, it is not enough simply to reach this goal, but what will you do with it once you are there?

Monetize it, of course!

After publishing thousands of books, I know for sure that the real money is not in the book royalties; it's in how you use your book to get high-paying clients, get speaking gigs, and build your business. Some of my clients have built multi-million-dollar businesses using the strategies I will teach you in the next few pages.

In this phase, you will learn how to extend the content of your book to build a profitable 7- or 8-figure business.
- How to leverage your book to land speaking engagements
- How to generate high-quality leads
- How to set your book up to win new business for you
- How to create a video course around your book

How to develop your own signature coaching program

Monetization: How To Leverage Your Book To Land Speaking Engagements

Publishing a book gives you a tremendous amount of influence and credibility. Admittedly, we are willing to pay to listen and learn from a bestselling author because we feel they have something important to say.

A professional speaker who has never published a book might be able to charge $500 to $5,000 for a single speech. Conversely, a speaker who is also a published author could easily command $10,000 to $50,000. Check out this [Best-Selling Business Author Speakers for Events | Key Speakers Bureau](#) to find out what published authors are charging per speaking gig.

On average, they are charging $25k+, including travel and hotel accommodations.

That's how powerful a book can be as a positioning and marketing tool. When it comes to spreading your ideas and message, nothing compares to a live, captive audience.

The best time to make the conference rounds as a paid speaker is as soon as your book makes it to the top of the bestseller list in your category.

So, you need to start planning for your live presentation early on to make sure you're ready to kickstart your public speaking journey.

5 Ways to Leverage Your Book to Land Speaking Gigs

1. *Update your online profiles.*

Add "Author" and the titles of your book in your profile, especially your LinkedIn profile, to reinforce your industry thought leader status. Include three to four sentences on who you are, what you speak about, and how you can help audiences with your message.

2.   Repurpose your book's content on social media.

Make it part of your content strategy to post small pieces of content, i.e., lists, quotes, 300-word posts, images, tweets, links, etc., with hashtags to spread the message of your book. This is a way for people to identify you as an expert in your field.

3.   Take advantage of events.

Attend and network with organizers of conferences in your industry.

Events are planned way in advance, and chances are you will have to wait three months to a year to land a speaking slot in your industry.

In the meantime, become an attendee and network with organizers and delegates. Instead of a business card, give your book to people you meet at the event.

You can find relevant events in your industry through online resources like eventbrite.com, meetup.com, and Facebook Events. Search for events happening nearby and join them to expand your network.

4.   Do "guest" rounds in podcasts.

Dig into your network of colleagues, peers, and influencers and propose guest appearances to podcasts as a resource speaker. This is a chance to spread your message, market your book, and impress listeners. In chapter 8.2, I explained in detail how you can find and get on relevant podcasts to promote your book, brand, and business.

5.   Talk to anyone willing to listen.

Whether it's an informal group meeting, an intimate dinner, or a one-on-one encounter, take every opportunity to engage someone in a conversation about your book.

This is how Simon Sinek became the most in-demand bestselling author and speaker on leadership.

The next person you talk to could lead you to a big speaking opportunity.

You can find the best speaking gigs in just 30 seconds with the help of [MySpeakingAgent](#), which gives you access to more than 1,000 contacts in the conference circles. This makes it easier for you to get booked for speaking gigs by knowing who to talk to.

Sign up for Agent by visiting [myspeakingagent.com](#).

Aside from connecting with conference decision-makers, enlist yourself and your bestselling book for speaking gigs.

Clients and promoters look for resource speakers for their digital and in-person events worldwide. The best option to make yourself discoverable is to sign up for speaking directories such as [Speakerhub](#), [Speakermatch](#), or [eSpeakers](#).

If you haven't done any speaking before, then you can start with $5k per speaking gig. Then, gradually, you can increase the price to $10k, $20k, and more.

I've got some clients who charge $50k+ per speaking gig, and usually, they do 2-3 engagements per month.

It could take 2-3 years to reach $50k+, but once you do it, $100k+ month won't be much more difficult.

Also, once you speak on the stage, you can offer your book for free, increasing your goodwill, and then you can enroll your audiences in your high-ticket programs.

That's what big brand names like Tony Robbins and Brendon Burchard do. They make millions of dollars through one speaking gig by selling their high-ticket programs to their audience.

So, the sky's the limit. If you do it correctly, building a multi-million-dollar business with speaking is definitely possible.

Monetization: How To Generate High-Quality Leads Using Your Book

Your status as a bestselling author will increase your premium, which means you can dictate your price and charge much more for your time. The key is using your newfound status to generate leads for your business or services.

When a reader purchases your book, you have the opportunity to collect their email and build your email list.

But why emails? Why not your social media accounts instead?

Studies show that the average ROI for an email is $44. That means for every $1 spent on email marketing, you will receive $44 in return.

In social media, there is no real way to track ROI. The methods used in different social media platforms for one brand do not necessarily work for another, making it hard to compare the ROI.

A good email list has many profitable things to offer:

1. You can promote your products and services directly to your audience, unlike in social media, where you have to go through a platform (Twitter, Facebook, LinkedIn, etc.) to access your audience.

In the case of an email list, you can send the message straight to your reader.

2. Emails are permission-based, meaning people give you their email addresses because they want to connect with you.

Your readers have already shown interest in you, your products, or your services, making it much easier for them to convert into customers or clients.

According to OptinMonster, the email conversion rate is 6.05%, while social media conversion rates are just 1.9%.

3. Promoting your books, coaching services, and other products is easy. Since you have permission to send information to your readers, you also get to talk about your promotions, sales, deals, and releases.

If your reader knows someone who needs this information, they can easily forward the email. You get free promotions while expanding your reach.

You can build your email list using your book with this lead generation sequence:

1. Create a lead magnet that supplements your book. A short eBook or a checklist will do. Include it as a bonus for purchasing your book.
2. Design a landing page and download page for your eBook or checklist.
3. For readers to claim their bonus or free giveaway, they will have to opt-in via a landing page link included in the book.

Here is an example of a lead magnet:

1. Set up your Email Campaign, which can look something like this:
   - Email No. 1 – Send a Thank You message with a short background about yourself.
   - Email No. 2 – Send your best works and testimonials. End with a promise of a gift in the next email.
   - Email No. 3 – Reveal your limited-time gift – an event invitation or a free consultation.

Pro Tip: Set up your lead generation funnel using [ClickFunnels](#) and pair it up with automated email marketing software like [ActiveCampaign](#).

In the next few pages, I will explain different strategies to monetize your email list in the following few pages.

Monetization: How To Set Your Book Up To Win New Business For You

You will become highly desirable as an expert by successfully positioning yourself with a book. Prospective clients will start to come for your advice instead of you selling to them.

There are several instances when publishing a successful book catapulted authors from anonymity to leading captains of industry. For example, Robert Kiyosaki, author of Rich Dad, Poor Dad, which has sold more than 27 million copies worldwide, was virtually unknown before his book.

His book grew his business into a knowledge empire worth over 80 million dollars in products, seminars, manuals, and digital content.

A great book can help you generate new leads and income streams for your venture like never before.

Six Things You Can Do with Your Book to Win New Business

1. *Publish your contact information in your book.*

Let your readers know that they can reach you long after reading your book by posting any contact information below.

This is an invitation to keep in touch and an opportunity to grow your email list. Include this info in the "About the Author" section at the end of the book:

- Booking link where they can schedule a call with you
- Events calendar where they can meet you in person
- Email address

- LinkedIn, Facebook, and Twitter handles
- Offer something for free in exchange for their email address
- Link to your business website

Do you know that you can continually update your manuscript on Kindle?

If you want to update the Author section of your book, you can easily do that. Just make the changes to your manuscript and re-upload the new file on Amazon KDP.

It's that simple.

That's one of the benefits of self-publishing an Amazon eBook.

2. *Start a book conversation on social media.*

Keep the conversation going about the ideas in your book by asking questions, running polls, or soliciting comments on your LinkedIn and Twitter accounts.

This is an opportunity to lead engaged readers to your business.

3. *Use your book as a business card.*

Before Dan Lok became a multi-million-dollar tycoon, he was a struggling first-time book author. He made the business conference rounds across cities and gave away his book to people he met.

Giving your book to new contacts is more impressive and memorable than handing them another boring business card.

4. *Use your book as a business case study.*

5. Write about success stories inspired by your content to convert readers into customers. Post them on your author blog with a link to your business site or include them in your next book. ***Offer your book for wholesale to relevant organizations.***

Make a case for how whole organizations (local or national, corporate or non-profit, educational, religious, etc.) can benefit from reading your book.

The 7 Habits of Highly Effective People, by Stephen Covey, positioned as a productivity training module, sold millions of copies through bulk orders from corporations.

6. Nurture your email list.

Send free, high-value content to your email list, i.e., whitepapers, case studies, checklists, and infographics.

Invite your prospect list to come see you in person or interact with you online.

Now, another thing you can do is to run Facebook ads to offer your book for free in exchange for their name, email, and phone number. Of course, that can cost money, but again, you can make a lot of money on the backend.

I easily make 25x more money than I spend on Facebook ads promoting my book.

Some of my clients also use the same funnel to build their email lists by running Facebook ads for their books.

The only downside to publishing your book on Amazon is you don't get your readers' contact information. That's why you can promote your book through Facebook ads and directly deliver it to their email once they provide their contact information.

Once you build an email list of engaged subscribers who are also your readers, they will see you as an authority on the topic or a celebrity.

You can offer them a free 15-minute or 30-minute consultation call (position it as that it's worth $1000 or more). They will be awestruck once they get on a call with you because they see you as a celebrity. They have read your book, and they are talking to its author.

Help them if they have any questions, and if you think they are a fit, you can also offer them your high-ticket coaching, consultation, video course, or service.

That's a great way to make tons of money in the backend. I've got several clients who use the same funnel to make 6 figures every month.

Monetization: How To Create A Profitable Video Course Around Your Book

Your bestseller is just a take-off point to expanding the reach of your philosophy and expertise. Two things can happen after this point: You fall off the cliff or climb higher. We'll discuss the many ways you can create programs and courses to sell at a premium.

Eventually, you might be too busy to attend every speaking engagement you're invited to. After all, you can't be in two places at once.

You will want to keep making money from your ideologies and expertise.

One of the great ways to do that is by creating seminars and video courses that live online and can be accessed on demand. Stemming from the ideas of your book, you can create courses, how-tos, and even seminars to sell to corporations and businesses to help their employees gain knowledge from your industry know-how.

But of course, the written word is vastly different from a live experience, so it helps to know what to expect when translating your bestseller into a training module.

Tone, focus, and specificity should be at the forefront of your course. Ideally, a better, more conversational, less rigid adaptation of your work is received.

Once you've focused on your training module, you can package this course and sell it to corporations who are interested. You can charge anywhere from $199 to $1,999 for your courses.

By linking to the course inside your book, readers can pay to access certain key ideas and programs through the video course.

Let's take a look at "Masterclass" by James Clear. The video course came from the topic mentioned in Clear's book, Atomic Habits, and was the world's best online course in forming good habits and breaking bad ones.

Bringing this closer to home, I have created courses to teach people how to write, publish, and market books since writing this book. In fact, more than 10,000 people have taken my courses, expanding my business and expertise and, ultimately, my revenue.

So, it is with confidence that I provide you with these steps to create your own online course:

1. Know what to teach.

Before you can build your own course, decide on the topic you want to teach. Remember these four criteria when deciding on a topic:

- **There is existing demand for the topic** – As we talked about early on, be sure to write about something people are interested in.
- **It solves a problem** – Your topic should be compelling enough for your audience to buy it.
- **It's something people want to learn from you** – As you build your authority with your book, your video course should be further proof of your expertise.
- **It is related to your book** – When you build your brand around your book, you can market different products inside the same brand.

Pro Tip: Ideally, you have already done all of the relevant research since this is one of the final steps in your publishing journey. But if you are considering creating a course before you have the book idea, be sure to go back and read Step 1 about Ideation.

2. Validate your idea.

It's not enough just to know what people want to learn. You also need to make sure that they are willing to pay to learn it.

Find out if your topic is profitable by seeding the idea that you'll be launching an online course soon.

Make an announcement in your email list, social media groups, and other places where your target audience hangs out.

- **Pre-sell your course**
  - Start marketing and promoting your course even if it's not yet complete. You can post publicly that you have something in store for your audience and will be opening the course soon.

- **Set up a free course**
  - Let people experience your online course on a small scale by giving them access to the first few parts of it. With this strategy, they will know the value they can get if they opt-in for the full course.

If people opt out, you can use that opportunity to ask them what their expectations are and what else they would want to know more about the course.

3. Start creating the course outline.

Now that you have discovered a profitable topic, start making the backbone of your course.

Be sure to identify what key ideas from the book will be most important to the students.

For example,

- What specific steps do they need to take to help them get closer to their goal?

- What skills do they need to learn?
- What actions do they need to take to solve the problem?

4. Begin creating the lessons of your course.

Break the ideas or steps into modules and individual lessons, making each digestible at between four and 10 minutes.

Create an action item, an assignment, a quiz, or a worksheet at the end of each module. This will help the students apply their learning and, at the same time, give them a win for every milestone acquired.

Remember to prioritize the quality of your topic over the delivery to ensure they can get the most value out of your course.

This step involves the following actions:
- Writing the courses
- Writing your scripts
- Recording the video course
- Editing the videos
- Uploading the course

There are several tools you can use to build your online course. My personal favorite is Skool. What I love about Skool is that it is so easy to navigate and you can host all your courses in one place. But the best part is you can build a community where people can communicate with each other. You can charge a monthly retainer to access the community and have weekly or bi-weekly group calls, and people can join it directly through Skool.

If you want to join AuthorsOnMission's Skool community, you can join it for free here.

With Skool, you can build an environment where your students can thrive together. Encourage them to interact, advise one another, and discuss their tasks. Regularly visit and comment on your students' posts. You can also start a contest to increase engagement within the group.

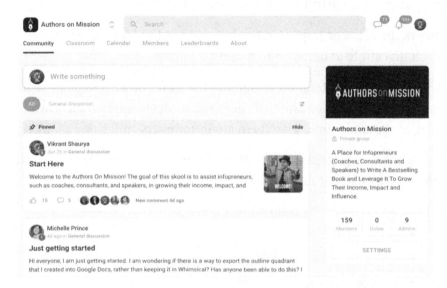

You don't need a professional camera and studio setup to record your video course. You can record videos through your laptop or your smartphone.

I usually record my courses through Loom and use a noise-canceling tool along with it: Krisp

5. Accommodating your first class of students.

Start opening your course to your first students while you continue to promote your course to a wider audience.

You can use your first students to learn what you must improve and what you need to add to your course. Don't forget to record your progress and get your students' honest feedback.

For example, you can sell your course for a 1-time fee of $999. That way, selling even 10 courses monthly is an easy $10k passive income for you.

Or you can do it for a monthly retainer of $99. While $99 per month might look small, once you build a community, people want to stay in the community. And even if you get 10 clients per month for this, after 10 months, you will be at around $10k per month, and after 20 months, $20k per month... The sky's the limit.

I have seen many authors who have built this kind of membership fee structure and are making $50k+ per month on passive income alone and you can easily build this type of membership on Skool.

Monetization: How To Develop Your Own High-Ticket Coaching Program

A topic in your book can be magnified into a coaching program that high-ticket clients can learn from. Through coaching, you can offer a premium service to a smaller number of people by leveraging your book's bestselling status and modern technology.

If your book does a good job of sustaining interest long after reading it, readers will seek you out for more of your expertise and will be willing to invest a premium for your time.

Think of your book as a commodity that costs readers less than $20 to purchase but ultimately is the key to getting high-ticket clients for maximum profit.

A coaching program is the start of a larger business relationship—a significant money and time investment for your client.

Think about how to scale the value of your content and ideas to be worth $3,000 or more each.

How to create a Signature Coaching program

A signature coaching program is a process you have developed based on your experiences and how you can help others.

You are willing to teach your discovered solution to let others achieve results, too. Of course, it is packaged in a way to create high-value, in-depth training.

Unlike other training materials, a signature coaching program has a more direct approach and focuses on the client's results. You have a higher engagement with your clients because you must regularly interact with them and follow their growth.

Let's discuss how you can create your own signature coaching program.

Step 1: Define the goal of your program.

Before you begin, you must be clear on what you want people to achieve by the end of the program. What specific results does the student expect to gain?

Step 2: Be clear about who your target students are.

Identify your target market. Try to narrow it down to a specific group of people that you want to teach.

It's easier to structure your program if you know who you are dealing with. What pain points do you want to help them resolve? What are their dreams and goals that you can help obtain?

Gaining clarity on your target students helps you understand where they are and how you can help them. This also helps you speak in their language.

Step 3: Give it a compelling title.

Decide on the title or name of your signature coaching program based on your book's topic. This is to maintain brand consistency across your products and services.

Make a catchy, attractive, and irresistible title that is easy to remember and has a deep connection to your book.

Step 4: Design your own coaching framework.

This is where you make your coaching program outline. Identify the main concepts and topics you should discuss.

Structure it with features that are unique compared to your competitors. Find your unique selling proposition (USP) so you can stand out from other similar coaching programs.

Step 5: Formulate specific instructions for every main topic.

In this step, you can now start creating your modules. These specific instructions, lessons, exercises, and other activities will ensure your clients achieve results.

It's the "how to" part of the program or the steps to reach the endpoint.

Step 6: Tell your success story.

This is the part where you display your expertise on the topic. Establish yourself as a "go-to" person and explain why people should seek your advice.

Based on your book, what specific topics do you want to be known for?

Step 7: Decide how long the program will be.

Your signature coaching program can run for 2, 4, 6 months, or even a year. Some coaches offer a 30-day or 90-day program.
Decide on the duration of the program, depending on the weight of the topic. Find out what works best for you and your clients.

Step 8: Surprise them with a bonus for finishing the program.

Add value to your clients by giving them a gift at the end of the program. This also helps them to stay motivated to finish the whole program.

Step 9: Price your services.

Find a price for your signature coaching program with which you are comfortable. Some experts can charge between $3k-$10k per month for their coaching programs.

You might want to try starting with $1k or $2k monthly. Once you get great testimonials and clients' results, you can increase your price to $3k, $5k, or even $10k.

You can also upsell your video course or membership students to your signature coaching program.

I have a client who is in DEI Space and has built a DEI consultation program, for which she charges $120k to her consulting clients. Her clients are big corporate executives, so $120k is nothing for them. She just takes 4-5 clients per month and makes around half a million dollars this way.

And remember everything started for her from the book.

Key Takeaways: Step 9 – Monetization

As you can see, writing a bestselling book is about more than simply getting your name out there as an author. The benefits of creating a profitable book that hits the bestseller list are far-reaching and can help define your career and set your life on a trajectory for success.

Whether you aspire to have a seven-figure business or write hundreds of books and be well-known as an author and influencer, the choice is yours.

Let's review the things we talked about in Step 9 about Monetization:

- How to leverage your book to land speaking engagements
- How to generate high-quality leads
- How to set your book up to win new business for you
- How to create a video course around your book
- How to develop your own signature coaching program

Achieving the status of bestselling author has helped launch my career and life to heights I had only imagined and I am so excited to help you do the same. Please reach out at

vikrant@authorsonmission.com and let me help you share about your book and all the many paths it is taking you on.

THREE MORE REASONS TO SELF-PUBLISH YOUR BOOK TODAY

What more can I say about the process of self-publishing?

Yes, it's a lot of hard work, but breaking into the world of publishing is no longer impossible like it once was.

Every single success starts with that one thought that could change your life. And publishing your book can take you to incredible new heights.

Here are three more reasons why you need to self-publish your book today:

1. Generate Investor Interest

Becoming a publishing success generates interest among business leaders and investors.

If you are looking for investment capital to grow your business, you can leverage your publishing experience to attract these influential leaders and get funding for your venture.

2. Get Like-Minded Collaborators and Partners

Becoming a bestselling author will align you with like-minded individuals who may want to partner with you in your current business or collaborate on a future partnership or endeavor.

3. Charge premium prices for your services

Your status as a bestselling author will up your premium, allowing you to name your price and charge much more for your time.

Ultimately, whether you're amid literary fame or simply trying to attract attention, your book can be the gateway to bigger and better things.

When it comes down to it, your book is like a business card or a brochure for your business. Use it to get that next great opportunity.

HELP ME HELP OTHERS WITH THIS BOOK

If you find this book helpful at all, please write a review so more people can find it. Simply go to

Authorsonmission.com/amazon-review

We're all searching for books to help improve our lives and businesses, and reviews are a huge source of influence when it comes to what people choose.

I know this book can positively impact many people as long as it gets some great reviews to help kick things off.

In addition to the power of a review, I also want to know personally how this book has helped you.

I print out every book review I get and hang them on my office wall to read for inspiration throughout the day. Your reviews validate my hard work and long hours invested spent writing.

Thank you again for reading this book and for all of your support so far. I'm truly honored and grateful.

If you have any questions or need any help on your publishing journey, email me directly at vikrant@authorsonmission.com and I'll be happy to help in any way I can.

See you on the bestseller list.

CONCLUSION

Now that we have covered all the topics on how to launch a book—from writing the manuscript to publishing and all the way to launch—it's time for you to implement what you have learned and reap its rewards.

There's a whole new world waiting for you to discover.

Many people have become successful after publishing their own books. Industry leaders like Robert Kiyosaki, Tim Ferris, Tony Robbins, Brendon Burchard, Eckhart Tolle, and Gary Keller have built their personal brands around their books.

They all optimized the power of their books to expand their network and scale their businesses.

The next big name could be yours.

The methods mentioned in this book have already been tested by my years of personal experience in writing a bestselling book from scratch.

It has also been proven by hundreds of people I have helped launch books and book series.

You don't have to go through the entire process of acquiring the knowledge and skills in book publishing. All my ideas, skills, and years of experience as a book publisher have been compressed into this book. All you have to do is implement the methods you've just learned about. What you have in your hands is a tested and proven plan to write, publish, market, and make a profit from your own book. I've already done the heavy lifting of trial and error, mistakes, and failures. The only thing for you to do now is take action.

"Without knowledge, action is useless, and knowledge without action is futile." — Abu Bakr

Knowledge and action go hand-in-hand in a successful book launch. If you go your own way of publishing a book without the knowledge to do so, you risk wasting a lot of time, effort, and money.

At the same time, knowing how to publish a book is not enough. You also need to do what the book instructs.

Publishing a book is just the beginning of a wonderful journey. What lies ahead after a book launches are opportunities for speaking engagements, getting clients worldwide, becoming an authority in your industry, and much, much more.

And it all begins with a single step: getting started.

I have personally tried and tested all the techniques mentioned in this book, and these are the exact steps my team and I have used to help many clients become bestselling authors with our [done-for-you service]().

If you have any questions or need help on your publishing journey, email me directly at [vikrant@Authorsonmission.com]().

Happy to help. I can't wait to see you on the bestseller list.

WHAT'S NEXT?

What you have learned from this book are the actual steps to writing, publishing, and marketing your book and using it to monetize.

What's next is simply putting this plan into action by checking off the items to get you closer to your goal of becoming a profitable author.

Self-publishing is a tremendous opportunity, and taking advantage of it has never been so easy. We live in this amazing knowledge economy where whole new streams of income are possible for authors.

Don't miss a step from *How to Write a Bestseller*. Secure your spot on the top of the bestseller list by downloading all the resources mentioned in the book.

Here's the direct link to download all your resources: Authorsonmission.com/resources

You'll automatically receive access to the list of tools and services I recommend as well as all the checklists and action items mentioned throughout this book.

You'll also be added to my popular weekly newsletter, where you will get the latest hacks and strategies to help you along your book-writing and publishing journey.

HOW TO WRITE A BESTSELLER

Authorsonmission.com

And there you have it!

A complete, step-by-step guide to self-publishing a bestseller and then using it to get clients, speaking gigs, and make a profit and an in-depth presentation of the entire process.

If you are seriously considering self-publishing, I recommend reading this book a few more times and paying special attention to the strategies, action plans, and key takeaways I laid out for you.

From my team at Authorsonmission.com, I thank you for picking up this book. This guide is meant to help set your author journey on a path to success.

This very same playbook has helped our clients achieve their life-long goals of becoming bestselling authors. But don't take our word for it.

Here's what they have to say –

"If you're thinking of writing, publishing or marketing your book, I highly recommend working with Authors On Mission."
John Chappelear
Changing The Focus
Author of The Daily Six

"Using this service really streamlines the book writing and publishing process. I highly recommend!"
Chrissa McFarlane
CEO, Patientory, INC.
Author of Future Women

"I'm really thankful to Vikrant and his team at Authors On Mission for helping me write my book."
Dr. John Burd
CEO, Lysulin and Wonder Spray

Author of The Natural Solution to the Diabetes Epidemic

"Thanks to the new book cover alone, I'm selling significantly more books now, without any other changes."
Terry Begue
Speaker
Author of Attract & Keep Customers For Life

"If you're looking for top-notch design for your own book project, I highly recommend reaching out to Authors On Mission.
Dr. Lusia Fomuso
Pharmacogenomics Expert
Author of Thank You, Essential Heroes

"We sold over a thousand copies the first week alone. Authors On Mission rocks!"
Vance Hilderman
CEO, AFuzion Incorporated
Author of The Aviation Development Ecosystem

"Their team, their process, their services are without a doubt, best in class and well worth the investment."
Mike Giaimo
Founder, Leverage Resources
Author of The Professional You

"With their help, I had sales out of this world. I became a number #1 bestselling author in three leadership categories."

Nicole Smith
CEO, JMS Creative
Author of 20 Golden Leadership Nuggets

"I'm thrilled and proud that my book became a number one bestseller on Amazon, thanks to the exceptional service from Authors On Mission."
Bruce Weddle
Sales Expert
Author of Master of One Call Close

"Thanks to Authors On Mission, I now have the social proof and the credibility and people all around the world being familiar with our story."
Meridith Alexander
Creative Talent Strategies, Inc.
Author of The Sky is the Limit

Following the same process and strategies mentioned in this book, I have helped thousands of clients turn their ideas into bestselling books with the help of our Done-For-You Book Writing, Publishing and Marketing service. Read more of our success stories at Authorsonmission.com.

This book is meant to help YOU share your ideas, stories, and experiences with the world. I truly believe in the power of books to transform lives. They have certainly transformed mine.

This book you just read, *How To Write A Bestseller*, is about helping you and helping your future readers.

In fact, the book inside your head right now could help thousands of people currently struggling and looking for answers. These people don't know it yet, but they need your book. And that's why you have to get it out there.

Want to know my book's vision? That's it.

Want to know my WHY? Yes, that is it.

Together, we can change the world for the better, one book at a time.

Before you close this book, please think back on what you just experienced:

- How did you find this book overall?
- Did it teach you something new?
- Was it worth reading?

If you find this book helpful, please write a review so more people can find it. Simply go to authorsonmission.com/amazon-review.

We're all searching for books to help improve our lives and businesses, and reviews greatly influence people's choices.

I know this book can positively impact many people as long as it gets some great reviews to help kick things off.

In addition to the power of a review, I want to know how this book has helped you personally.

I print out every book review I get and hang them on my office wall to read for inspiration throughout the day. Your reviews validate my hard work and the long hours invested in writing.

Thank you again for reading this book and for your support so far. I'm truly honored and grateful.

If you have any questions or need any help on your publishing journey, email me directly at vikrant@authorsonmission.com, and I'll be happy to help in any way I can.

If you have any thoughts about how I could improve this book, I'd love to hear them, too.

And, of course, if you plan to follow these steps and write your own book, I'd love to be a part of your journey.

Please reach out to me at vikrant@authorsonmission.com.

I personally read and answer all my emails.

Happy writing, and I hope to see you on the bestseller list.

Vikrant Shaurya
Founder, CEO
Authors On Mission

YOUR FREE GIFT

To thank you for buying this book, I'm offering this FREE gift (1-page Bestseller Checklist) exclusive to you for trusting *How to Write a Bestseller* with your book's future.

You'll also get access to a collection of printable book-writing, publishing, and marketing checklists and other resources mentioned in this book.

Visit authorsonmission.com/gift to get free instant access.

Produce

1. IDEATION
- ✓ Book Idea
- ✓ WHY
- ✓ Target Reader
- ✓ Hook
- ✓ Outline

2. WRITING
- ✓ Research
- ☐ Title & Subtitle
- ✓ Introduction
- ✓ Rough Draft
- ✓ Conclusion

3. EDITING
- ✓ Content Editing
- ✓ Line-by-Line Editing
- ✓ Verbal Read-Through
- ✓ Copyediting
- ✓ Proofreading

Publish

4. POSITIONING
- ☐ Description
- ☐ Acknowledgement
- ☐ Author Bio
- ☐ Author Photo
- ✓ ISBN

5. DESIGN
- ✓ Kindle Cover
- ✓ Paperback Cover
- ✓ eBook Formatting
- ✓ Paperback Formatting
- ✓ Book Trailer

6. DISTRIBUTION
- ☐ Amazon KDP Account
- ☐ Profitable Categories
- ✓ Profitable Keywords
- ☐ Kindle and Paperback on KDP
- ☐ Audiobook on ACX

Profit

7. LAUNCH
- ✓ Amazon Author Central
- ✓ Initial Reviews
- ✓ #1 Best-seller Spot
- ✓ More Sales and Downloads
- ✓ More Reviews

8. MARKETING
- ✓ Author Website
- ✓ Press and Media Coverage
- ✓ Social Media Marketing
- ✓ Paid Ads
- ✓ Influencers' Platform

9. MONETIZATION
- ✓ Speaking Opportunities
- ✓ Get New Clients
- ✓ Lead Generation
- ✓ Video Course
- ✓ Coaching Program

ABOUT THE AUTHOR

Vikrant Shaurya is the CEO and the creative mind behind Authors On Mission. His passion for storytelling led him to become a bestselling author and now he helps others do the same.

At Authors On Mission, Vikrant and his team help entrepreneurs, coaches, consultants, speakers, and thought leaders turn their ideas into successful books.

He believes everyone has a story worth sharing and dedicates his work to making these stories heard. With 1,000+ clients who've become bestselling authors through Authors On Mission's done-for-you book writing, publishing, and marketing services, Vikrant continues to inspire and empower aspiring writers to achieve their publishing dreams.

Send him an email directly at vikrant@authorsonmission.com and connect with him on LinkedIn at linkedin.com/in/vikrantshaurya.

Schedule a call with Authors On Mission's team here if you have a book idea and need professional help and support to get it done.

Made in the USA
Las Vegas, NV
22 September 2024